BUS LINE

A GIFT FOR GIVING

A GIFT FOR GIVING

MAKING *the* MOST *of the* PRESENT

BY DONNA LANG

PHOTOGRAPHS BY GEORGE ROSS

CLARKSON POTTER/PUBLISHERS
NEW YORK

To all of my dear friends

with whom I have exchanged gifts.

Thank you for sharing your bounty

and your creativity.

You have made gift giving so very

special to me

ALSO BY DONNA LANG

MAKE IT WITH STYLE SERIES:
DRAPERIES AND SWAGS
WINDOW SHADES
SLIPCOVERS

WITH LUCRETIA ROBERTSON:
DECORATING WITH FABRIC
DECORATING WITH PAPER

The publisher gratefully acknowledges permission to reprint text from the book *Creating Affluence*, © 1998 by Deepak Chopra. Reprinted by permission of Amber-Allen Publishing, Inc., P.O. Box 6657, San Rafael, CA 94903. All rights reserved.

Published by Clarkson Potter/Publishers, New York, New York. Member of the Crown Publishing Group.

Random House, Inc. New York, Toronto, London, Sydney, Auckland
www.randomhouse.com

Printed in China

Library of Congress Cataloging-in-Publication Data
Lang, Donna.
A gift for giving : making the most of the present / by Donna Lang.—1st ed.
Includes bibliographical references and index.
1. Handicraft. 2. Gifts. I. Title.
TT157.L25 2000
745.5—dc21 99-059906

ISBN 0-609-60590-9

10 9 8 7 6 5 4 3 2 1

First Edition

acknowledgments

Giving gifts is such a joyous activity. The whole process of writing this book has been enhanced by the contributions of many extraordinary people. Thank you one and all for sharing your talents with me: George Ross, Maryellen Stadtlander, and Lewis Bloom for taking such beautiful pictures; Susan Voigt Reising for her special insights and friendship; Karen Stadtlander for patiently working with me to wrap gifts and polish the manuscript; Jennifer Napier for the stylish book design; Tiina Dodenhoff for her clandestine visits to help; Pam Krauss and Chloe Smith for editing the book; Jane Treuhaft and Caitlin Daniels for design assistance; Susan Ginsburg and Susan Webman, super agent and super client; and Madeline, Ian, and Katie Hooper and Anne Heller for sharing their homes and gardens as photography locations. Also heartfelt thanks to Roberto and the staff at J & M Plant for having the perfect flowers, and Ellie Schneider and Catherine Horton for always having the right Offray ribbon for every gift-giving occasion.

contents

introduction

Let's face the facts together: Gift giving has changed. In today's world, we have a real responsibility not to clutter other people's lives with things they neither need nor want. We have a responsibility to think creatively about the gifts we give to the people we love, to the people we like, and to the people who cross our paths and make our days easier and better. Yet all too often we end up with the uncomfortable sense that we've chosen the wrong thing, spent too much money, saddled the recipient with one more item to tuck out of sight in an already overcrowded closet.

"CREATE WEALTH AND SPEND IT. SPEND IT LAVISHLY AND THEN SHARE IT AND GIVE IT TO OTHERS. GIVE IT TO YOUR CHILDREN, TO YOUR FAMILY, TO YOUR RELATIVES, TO YOUR FRIENDS, TO SOCIETY, AND TO THE WORLD. FOR WEALTH IS OF THE UNIVERSE AND IT DOES NOT BELONG TO US—WE BELONG TO IT."

—Deepak Chopra, M.D.

Flowers are always a welcomed gift, but you can make your floral gifts more special by personalizing your presentation. The lavish bouquet at left is created with hydrangea, larkspur, sweetheart roses, and green viburnum clustered in a flower market container that can be used over and over.

A Gift for Giving is the means to a new beginning. It is neither a gift book nor a gift-wrapping book; it is, rather, a gift-giving book—a happy combination of thoughtful gift ideas and wonderfully imaginative presentations that will enhance the recipient's life instead of imposing on it.

To give a gift is one of life's greatest joys. It's a tangible and direct way to share your sentiments, to show someone you care. Gift giving is a rich opportunity to bring pleasure not only to the recipient but to you, the giver, as well.

When framing money as a gift, choose a frame that reflects the style of the recipient. Will they respond to classic silver, natural wood, or contemporary metal? Once the money is spent, they will have a special frame to remind them of your generosity.

No one is perfect—I'm not, you're not—but we all want to find and give the perfect gift. How do you choose the perfect gift for a particular person? Start by asking yourself the following:

- What is *special* about this person?
- What would be special *to* this person?
- What would he *love* to have?
- What does she *wish* she had?
- What does he *need*?
- What does she *never have enough of*?
- What needs *replacing*?
- What would make him *laugh*?
- What are her *interests* or *passions*?
- What would he enjoy *tasting* or *smelling* or *seeing*?
- What would she love to *read* or *learn*?

When you begin to think of gift giving in this very personal way, finding the answer to the question "What shall I give?" becomes an exciting process of matching the gift, and its wrapping, to the recipient. Panic over gift giving disappears completely when you shift your mind-set *away* from that overwhelming fear of failure (yours) and turn it *toward* eliciting a joyful and appreciative response (theirs). Remember that gift giving is not necessarily about finding something large or fancy or expensive; it's about discovering the *right* gift, even if it's small, simple, or inexpensive. Truly, it's the generous *thought* that counts most.

THE SIX BASICS OF SUCCESSFUL GIFT GIVING

Keep these important points in mind when you think about gifts, and you'll never go wrong.

1

GIVE STRESS-FREE GIFTS. Don't give gifts that simply clutter up another person's life, because clutter turns to stress when it has to be stashed, taken care of, or gotten rid of. It's a lot more thoughtful to give a gift that can be consumed, recycled, or cherished for a lifetime. Food, flowers, money to buy a needed item—these gifts will afford pleasure without burden.

2

GIVE WITH AN OPEN HEART. A gift given grudgingly is no gift at all. If it's hard for you to give, think about what's holding you back. Perhaps this is the moment to divest yourself of the bad old rules of gift giving, and take to heart—an open heart—a realistic, more genuine approach to the subject. Dedicate only the time, money, and effort that you *want* to, and you'll find a new pleasure in giving.

3

IT REALLY *IS* THE THOUGHT THAT COUNTS. Let's stop confusing *value* with *expense*. Sometimes simple gifts well thought out are far more welcome, appropriate, and lasting (in memory) than grand gestures unaccompanied by true caring. Share a favorite recipe, poem, photo, meal. Give a posy of wildflowers. Pass along a good book. Give your time, skill, or service. Present your gift with imagination, and it will be priceless to the recipient.

4

BUY GIFTS ONE AT A TIME. The gift you give is not for someone in general, so don't buy generic one-gift-fits-all presents. Honor that special person by envisioning his or her hopes, dreams, goals, life experiences, likes, and dislikes. If you know that your dear friend aspires to learn the art of French cooking, show her that you support her: Give her a handsome copper mixing bowl and wire whisk or, even better, a series of classes at a culinary institute. Tailor your gift to fit the person, and be sure to make the presentation an integral part of the gift.

5

THINK OUT-OF-THE-BOX. It might be easiest to buzz over to the Gap and pick up a T-shirt for your friend's birthday, but does she really need another one? Maybe she's more in need of an evening out, with good music and enough time for a heart-to-heart talk with you. Expand your thinking about presents and the people to whom you give them. Get past the obvious and the easy.

6

GIVE GIFTS JUST BECAUSE . . . Don't wait for a birthday or a formal occasion to give a gift. Show your appreciation anytime—to friends, relatives, neighbors, teachers, bus drivers, anyone who makes a positive difference in your life. Your offering need not be large or splashy, but it should come from the heart. A favorite CD, a bottle of wine, a batch of chocolate chip cookies, or special soaps are lovely tokens for a "just because" moment.

Trust yourself: You have excellent intuition and a deep desire to share your good feelings with your loved ones. You'll find, wrap, and give the perfect gift, with *A Gift for Giving* to inspire and assist you.

I have been fortunate as an adult to have a circle of close friends whom I have known for many, many years. One of the ways we have always demonstrated our fondness for one another has been through the exchange of gifts, even in the leaner days when ingenuity was of necessity the most notable component of our presents. Now our budgets are less stringent and our time is at a premium; a quick stop at the department store would certainly be the path of least resistance. But I've learned that the personalized, lovingly conceived, and thoughtfully presented gifts of those early years still have the greatest impact and more than justify the time and effort I invested.

From my friends, and from all the gifts I've given and received in the past, I've learned that sentiment, not stuff, is what fills us with delight. So most of my gift giving is based on consumables—useful or lovely things that give the recipients a lift . . . and make no further demands on them. For this I generally choose from among four major categories of gifts: money, flowers, food, and what I call gifts of experiences—time to indulge a hobby, revel in relaxation, or enjoy a novel entertainment. In the chapters that follow I explore each of these categories in more depth, offering unique ways to package up the presents as well. If you make your selection from one of these groups, you are certain to bestow gifts that make both you and the recipient happy.

Here are a few of the simplest, most effective things you can do to help yourself toward carefree gift giving.

- TAKE NOTES. Use the Personal Gift Registry in the back of this book for jotting down bits of information about family and friends. Keep track of color preferences, sizes, favorite authors and music, hobbies, favorite foods, and any terrific gift ideas that pop into your head throughout the year. Think in terms of fantasies and memories too, not simply material things.

- BE PREPARED. Buy boxes, containers, wrapping paper, cards, ribbons,

OPPOSITE. Crisp, juicy red apples are the essence of autumn, a scrumptious gift for any family. Buy a handsome natural splint basket and fill it with delicious fruit; add a wonderful apple corer or paring knife. Personalize your gift even more by creating a special tag to complete the presentation (see sidebar, page 112).

and tie-ons wherever and whenever you find ones you like. Stash them in your gift wrap pantry (page 102) for future use.

- KEEP YOUR EYES OPEN. Be on the lookout for gifts and wrapping supplies that remind you of a special person. Label them with her name, record the purchases in your gift registry, and put them away in your gift wrap pantry to await the right moment.
- WATCH THE CALENDAR. Note birthdays, anniversaries, and other important dates as soon as you begin a new calendar or daybook. If you prefer, an e-mail service or software program can do this for you. Or get yourself an electronic organizer and let it do the job.
- USE CATALOGS. As catalogs arrive, tear out or mark interesting pages, and keep them in a file folder. (Be sure to note your customer number and the toll-free order number if it's not on the torn-out page.) Even if you don't actually purchase anything from catalogs, you'll find they're full of great gift (and gift-wrapping) ideas.

Keep a stash of these enchanting Chinese paper lanterns for presenting lightweight gifts such as scarves, ties, or jewelry.

Make two holes near the opening at the top of the lantern, and attach a length of cord, knotting the ends on the inside of the lantern. Remove the skimpy tassel that came with the lantern and replace it with a bigger, fuller purchased tassel.

With so many people editing their possessions, you can make *your* gifts most welcomed by choosing to give money, which allows the recipient to select his or her own gift, or consumable or recyclable choices of food or flowers. Or instead of rushing out to buy an object, stop a moment and think of giving an experience—a walking tour of historic buildings, audiotapes of a classic novel, or an evening at a comedy club.

Consider giving one big gift a year instead of squandering money on small items. Invest in something really special or in an experience that the recipient really wants. You can then give a card or a single flower or a small edible to mark each occasion throughout the year.

Once you have a great gift idea, I'll help you make the presentation as special as the gift. You'll be able to seamlessly integrate the selection of presents with imaginative ideas to enhance the experience of giving and receiving for all concerned. It's a pleasure for me to share these cherished gift concepts from my personal experience, including an array of options for personalizing your gifts to suit their honored recipients.

Getting the Most from Catalogs

Catalogs are a wonderful source of ideas for gifts and gift wraps. You may or may not actually order merchandise from the catalogs that arrive in your mailbox, but by the time you're finished looking at them, you'll have a good idea of what's available in the marketplace. And keep in mind that catalog and even Internet shopping can be a time-saver. In most cases you can place an order at any hour of the day or night, and if you're unhappy with your purchase most companies will allow you to return it for a full refund.

Keep on top of the influx of catalogs by quickly tearing out pages that may interest you later; stash them in a file until you have time for serious looking. Remember to jot down on torn-out pages your customer number and the 800 number for ordering. If you don't receive many catalogs, Post-it flags are a convenient way to mark pages and items that catch your eye. Take catalogs with you when you know you'll be spending some time in a holding pattern—waiting for the doctor, the Little League game, or car inspection.

As you find appropriate gifts for the people on your gift list, remember to record your ideas in your personal gift registry. At the back of this book you will find a prototype page that can be duplicated to create a loose-leaf notebook . . . or you may choose to develop your own format for record keeping. If you're very computer literate, you may want to store your records that way.

The Resource Guide offers suggestions for starting your gift search. It also includes space for you to add your own personal favorites to keep all information in one easy-to-find place.

COOKIES

1

giving money

NOTHING BUT HONEY IS SWEETER THAN MONEY.
—*Benjamin Franklin*

Remember the thrill of receiving a crisp twenty-dollar bill for your tenth birthday or a one-dollar bill under your pillow from the tooth fairy? It's a feeling we never truly outgrow, whatever our age (or bank account). A gift of "free" money is a gift of possibilities, a license to splurge on whatever you desire at the very moment you dream of it—a glamorous lunch with a friend, an expensive new lipstick, a soothing massage. And if *you* delight in receiving a little (or a lot) of mad money, you can be sure others do, too! In fact, a gift of cash is like two gifts, because it gives pleasure twice: when it's

An attractive new jar (or a funky flea-market find) filled with cash is a perfect gift for a new couple or a recent graduate in her first apartment. Find an attractive cookie jar—old or new, any style you think would suit your recipient—and fill it with cash for a rainy day or for little luxuries.

ABOVE AND BELOW. This fast, fun, and easy presentation will be especially appreciated by everyone on your list. Simply roll up bills of any denomination and slide them into balloons *before* they're inflated with helium.

A bouquet of three, five, seven, or nine translucent balloons looks great, and you might want to give the recipient a gold or silver kilt pin (a giant safety pin) to help her pop open her gifts.

Two things to remember: helium balloons begin to lose their buoyancy within a few hours of being filled, so plan accordingly. And translucent balloons may turn opaque when exposed to the sun, so keep them under wraps until you're ready to make your presentation.

received and when it's spent.For those with very specific tastes in, say, music or clothing—people for whom you wouldn't attempt to choose—cash is the perfect gift. They'll buy exactly what they want, and thank you for it. You may even want to make gifts of cash a tradition with friends or relatives—especially with children, students, young marrieds on tight budgets, and older folks on fixed incomes.

Giving money doesn't mean simply writing a check or stuffing a bill in a purchased card; money can be wrapped or presented as creatively and thoughtfully as any other gift. I have ideas for giving money to *everyone* on your list, for *any* occasion, and in *whatever amount* you choose. These fun and witty presentations will transform money from the gift of last resort, to the gift of first choice.

It has become a custom for me to "surprise" my dear friend Judy each birthday with money. After twenty years, the surprise, of course, is all in the presentation. It's fun for both of us. Each year I enjoy creating a new presentation, and Judy knows she'll have a little "mad money" to splurge on a special antique or new piece of jewelry.

You will find that this project can be adapted for virtually any gift-giving occasion. Changing the cover design tailors the gift for each recipient. Choose lacey paper and doilies for the new bride and groom; a rattle and bottle-printed paper for a baby gift; a sports design for a baseball fanatic; or classic leather and marble paper as a retirement gift. Directions for this patent-pending project follow on pages 25–26.

Remember, too, that money has more than one face. Foreign currency can make a wonderful gift for the traveler. I know a thoughtful aunt who gives this exotic treat each time a niece or nephew is planning a first trip abroad. A gift of currency from the country they will visit helps familiarize them with the monetary system, and gives them pocket money for their trip.

Finally, if you feel uncomfortable about giving money because the recipient will know exactly what you spent, go back and reread the pros of giving money. You'll probably find at least a few people on your gift list who would find a gift of money the most luxurious gift of all!

How much should you give?

Consider the following: How much would you spend on another sort of gift? Will you be giving the same amount to, for example, all six of your grandchildren? What would you like the recipient to be able to do with the money? Buy a book? A pair of earrings? A new car? What does your budget allow? Remember, whatever amount you decide on, large or small, it's the thought that counts.

Once you've decided on a gift of money, don't simply resort to a check or purchased money folder. Money can be wrapped and given as creatively and thoughtfully as any other gift. Here are a few points to keep in mind when making up your gift:

- Money comes in a variety of useful forms—rolls of dimes or quarters, bus tokens, subway cards, long-distance calling cards. These are all excellent gift choices.
- Gifts of cash are handsomest when the bills are crisp and new, so call your bank to request them in advance. Automated teller machines often dispense new bills, but your choice of denominations will be limited.
- Money has more than one face: Foreign currency is a wonderful gift for a traveler. Check local banks and currency exchange outlets to find what you need for the appropriate country.

The suggestions that follow are appropriate for gifts of ten up to one hundred dollars or more. But no matter what the monetary value, they all convey a message of creativity and caring.

Even a lettuce-hater will love this bowl of greens. Simply crumple twenty-five or more crisp new bills, toss them into a good-looking salad bowl, and add tongs. If you're transporting the gift, wrap it in clear cellophane and tie it with a pretty ribbon.

AMERICA
92670749 A
WASHINGTON, D.C.

Nöte Päd

banknote pad

A thick, bountiful pad of peel-off bills is an unforgettable present for anyone, young or old. Fifty or a hundred one-dollar bills make a very impressive stack, and the hot glue used to secure one end of the stack won't harm the cash one bit.

The instructions below apply to a stack of up to one hundred bills.

what you'll need

- Crisp new one-dollar bills in the desired quantity
- Lightweight cardboard: 1 piece 2⅝″ × 6 3/16″, for the backing; 2 pieces, each 2⅞″ × 6⅝″, for the front and back; 1 piece 2⅞″ high and as wide as the depth of the stack of bills, for the spine (For a stack of 100 bills, the spine width will be ⅝″; for 50 bills, the width will be 5/16″.)
- 2 binder clips
- Hot glue gun and glue stick
- 1 piece of marbleized or other decorative paper 3¾″ × 15″, for the cover
- Spray adhesive
- 1 piece of solid color or contrasting paper 2½″ × 13¼″, for the liner
- Contrasting paper, 3¾″ long, for embellishing the spine (optional)
- 2 pieces of double-face ribbon, each 9″ long, for the ties
- Metallic marker or press-on letters

how to do it

1. Square up the stack of bills and the cardboard backing piece. Secure them with the binder clips very close to the left end. Using the glue gun, apply hot glue to the end of the stack, covering the entire surface. Set aside.

NO GLUE GUN? NO PROBLEM!

You can make the Banknote Pad even without a glue gun. Buy one or two glue sticks and melt them in a double boiler on the stove or in a metal pan in a toaster oven. Carefully dip the left edge of your clipped-together bills and cardboard backing, just touching the edges to the melted glue.

If you melt the glue stick in a pot or pan, the excess glue will often harden when cool and release easily for disposal. To be on the safe side, however, you may want to use a disposable container, such as a coffee can.

2. Place the piece of decorative paper on a flat surface wrong side up and line up the cardboard front, spine, and back on it, allowing 1⁄16″ between pieces for the folds. Outline with pencil. Remove the cardboard pieces and spray the paper with adhesive. Replace the pieces and press firmly onto the paper.
3. Clip the corners of the paper on the diagonal. Fold the excess paper over onto the back of the cardboard pieces, making neat corners.
4. To make the ties, use hot glue to tack 1⁄2″ of one ribbon in place at one end of the cover, centered, as shown in the illustration; repeat with the second ribbon at the other end of the cover.
5. If you're embellishing the spine with contrasting paper, use spray adhesive to attach it, neatly centered, over the spine area. Fold excess paper onto the inside of the cover.
6. Apply spray adhesive to the wrong side of the solid color or contrasting liner paper. Center it over the inside of the cover and press firmly. Gently fold the cover to create the spine.
7. With a marker or press-on letters, write an appropriate message on the front of the cover. Add any extra touches that you've planned.
8. Hot-glue the cardboard back of the money stack inside the cover, centered neatly on the right. Close the pad and tie the ribbons in a bow.

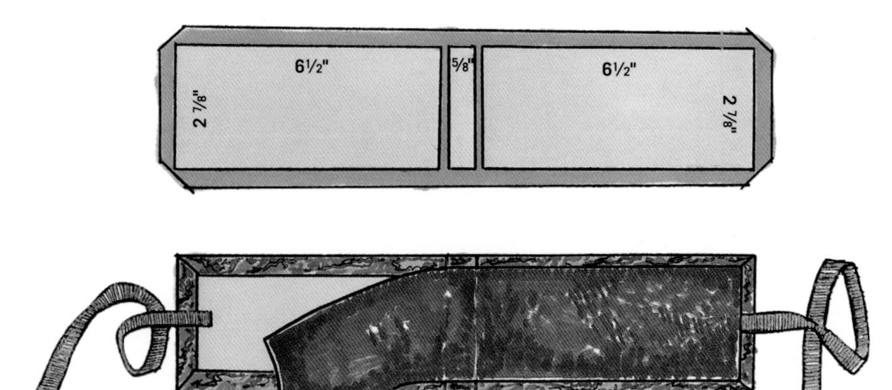

Note Pad
A 34721401K
$100
Ones
PILOT
GOLD MARKER
EXTRA FINE POINT

money tree

Money may not grow on trees, but this one is blooming with fan-folded offerings. Choose a large plant or a small tree that's appropriate for indoor use or outdoor planting, according to the recipient's situation. (Don't hesitate to opt for an artificial tree if that's what makes the most sense in your case.)

Noteworthy Sentiments

MONEY REALLY DOES GROW ON TREES!

Or for a retiree:

MAY YOUR RETIREMENT YEARS BLOSSOM WITH HAPPINESS.

what you'll need

- pot
- tree or plant (real or silk)
- moss
- crisp new paper money
- floral wire

how to do it

1. Pick a great-looking terra-cotta pot or other decorative container for the tree; if the tree is real, allow enough room for the roots and some growth, and include a matching saucer to catch the water.
2. Place the tree in the chosen pot, and cover the dirt (or the base, if you're using an artificial tree) with moss. Fold the bills accordion style, making 1/4" folds. Twist a short length of wire around each folded bill, 1/2" from the end, to make fans. Wire the fans to the tree.
3. If you like, make origami cranes instead of fans: Tape two bills together and fold one side under to make a square. Following the directions in any origami book, fold the square into a crane. Make several cranes, twist wire around the tail of each one, and attach them to the tree for a stunning effect.

nest eggs

Create a whimsical nest egg for a special someone by filling an empty nest with cash-stuffed painted eggs. Your nest can be as rich as you choose: a few dollars in coins for a small child or several hundred dollars in bills for an adult child who's leaving the nest.

what you'll need

- Hot glue gun and glue stick
- Craft store bird's nest
- Small forked branch
- One or more two-part hollow eggs, clear or opaque
- Acrylic craft paint in one or more colors
- Small flat paintbrush
- Coins or paper money in the desired amount
- Sprigs of ivy or other greenery for decoration

how to do it

1. Hot-glue the nest to the forked branch.
2. Paint the eggs with two coats of paint, allowing an hour for drying between coats. If the eggs are clear, paint the insides; if they are opaque, paint the outsides. To make authentic-looking robin's eggs using clear eggs, paint specks of rusty brown paint on the inside of the eggs before applying the first coat of pale blue paint; with opaque eggs, simply add the rusty brown specks when the second coat of pale blue is dry.
3. Fill the eggs with coins or neatly folded paper money, and arrange the eggs in the nest. Using hot glue, embellish the nest with sprigs of ivy or greenery.

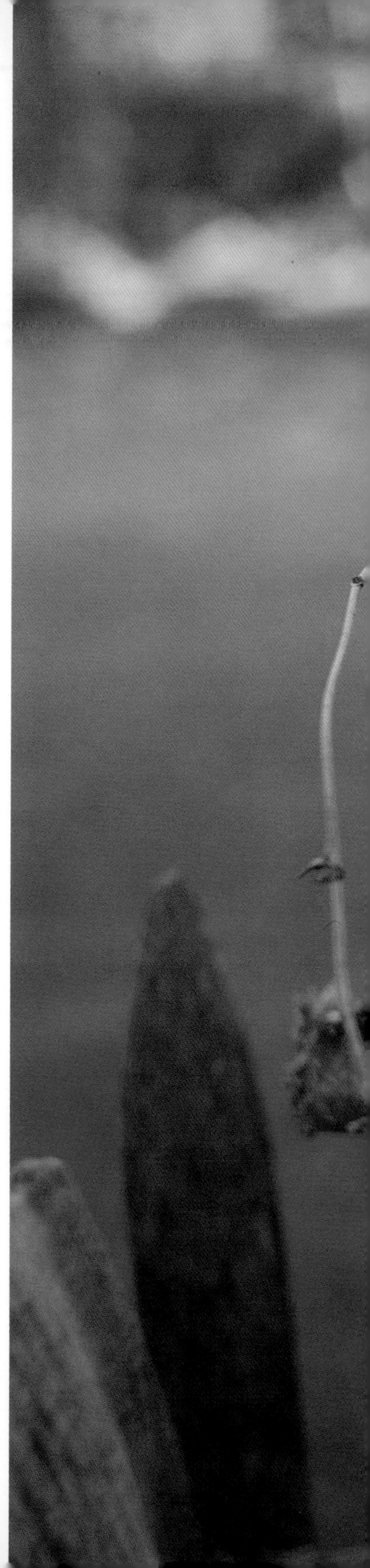

POND
SHED

buried treasure

Here, finding the gift is half the fun! It's easy to create an exciting treasure hunt for children or adults: Bury the loot in the backyard, in the sandbox, in a hollow tree, or under a bush. Make a parchment map (with charred edges for authenticity) leading to a canvas sack filled with cash, present your treasure hunter with the map and a small shovel, and send him off. If rainy weather prevents you from burying the treasure outdoors, hide it inside and substitute a child's sandbox shovel to carry out the theme.

what you'll need

- 8½″ × 11″ piece of parchment paper for the map, plus an extra piece
- Black or brown marker; fabric marker for the sack (optional)
- Match, lighter, or lit candle
- Twine or cord
- 12″ × 40″ piece of light canvas
- Needle and thread or sewing machine
- Paper money or coins, or both
- Small shovel

how to do it

1. On the parchment paper, draw your treasure map, marking the treasure with a big *X*. Add a compass to indicate direction. On the *extra* piece of parchment, try charring the edges with a match, lighter, or lit candle. When you can control the effect, char the edges of your map. Roll up the map and tie with a short length of twine or cord.
2. To make the money sack, fold the canvas in half lengthwise, right sides together, to make a rectangle 12″ × 20″. Stitch down the long sides, allowing ½″ for the seam. Press open the seams. Fold the top down 4″, wrong sides together, and press. Turn the sack right side out. If you like, use the green fabric marker to draw a big dollar sign on the sack.
3. Put the money in the sack and tie the opening with twine or cord. Bury the sack at the spot shown on the map. Present the recipient with the rolled-up map and the shovel.

If you're not good at mapmaking, invent a treasure hunt with clues written on strips of parchment paper. For kids, attach a little toy to each clue. Each clue leads to the hiding place of the next clue; the last clue leads to the treasure.

Shiny coins make an extra-special treasure. Clean grimy coins by dropping them into a glass of cola and letting them soak until clean. Rinse and wipe with a soft cloth.

the quarterly report

Anyone who's been caught at a telephone booth, a vending machine, or a Laundromat without the right change knows the value of a good stock of quarters, so here's a snappy way to present a generous supply of those useful coins.

A standard coin-collecting sheet, which measures 7⅜″ × 9⅛″, holds six dollars' worth of quarters; the number of pages (coin sheets) in your quarterly report will be determined by the amount of money you're giving. The directions here are based on a three-page booklet; adjust the measurements as necessary.

what you'll need

- Corrugated paper, 9¾″ × 19½″
- Glue for paper
- Paper for the title page and for the label
- 3 or more coin-collector's sheets for quarters
- Paper punch
- 22″ piece of rawhide
- Quarters to fill the coin sheets

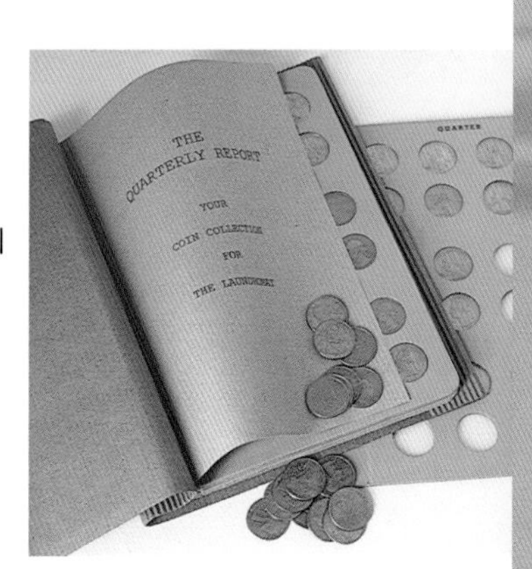

how to do it

1. Fold back 1¼″ at both short ends of the corrugated paper and glue.
2. On your computer or by hand create a 7⅜″ × 9⅛″ title page for the report. Using a coin-collector's sheet as a guide, punch two holes along the left edge of the title page. Make a 4″ × 4¾″ label in the same style as the title page and set aside.
3. To make the holes in the corrugated paper cover, first wrap it around the three coin pages and mark the placement of the holes on the front and back. Punch holes at the marks.
4. Align the holes in the cover, title page, and the coin pages, and thread the rawhide up through the holes. Tie on top with a double knot. Center and glue the label to the cover. Insert the quarters in the coin sheets.

THE
QUARTERLY
REPORT

HAIL A CAB ON ME!

money folders

Small unaccustomed luxuries are welcome gifts, and this is a gift that shouts, "Hail a cab (or take a bus or train) on me!" Tuck a few (or many) bills into a smart yellow-and-black folder, top with a toy taxi, and tie on a whistle for fun. Although this gift was created to give money for a specific use, the custom money folder can be adapted for any occasion. The basic directions will be the same; just change the colors and the message.

what you'll need

- 1 sheet of black paper 8½″ × 11″, for the folder
- 1 sheet of bright yellow paper 8½″ × 11″, for the liner
- Glue for paper
- Broad-nibbed white marker
- Crisp new bills in the desired quantity
- Model taxicab
- ⅜″ wide ribbon
- Whistle with ring

how to do it

1. To make the folder, first cut the black paper according to the diagram; then cut out an oval to allow the face of a bill to show through. Fold in the side tabs and apply glue to the tops of the tabs. Fold the cutout section up over the tabs and press to adhere.
2. To make the liner, first print your message (by hand or computer) on the upper half of the yellow paper. Cut the paper down to 7½″ × 6½″ and fold in half. The liner is now 7½″ wide, each half is 3¼″ high, and the message is centered in the top half. Slip the bottom half of the liner into the folder, apply glue to the back of the top half, and press it in place against the folder.
3. Use the marker to draw a double white line on the top of the black folder.
4. Tuck the bills inside the folder, with a face showing through the oval cutout. Put the taxi on top of the closed folder and tie the ribbon around both, adding the whistle as you make the knot.

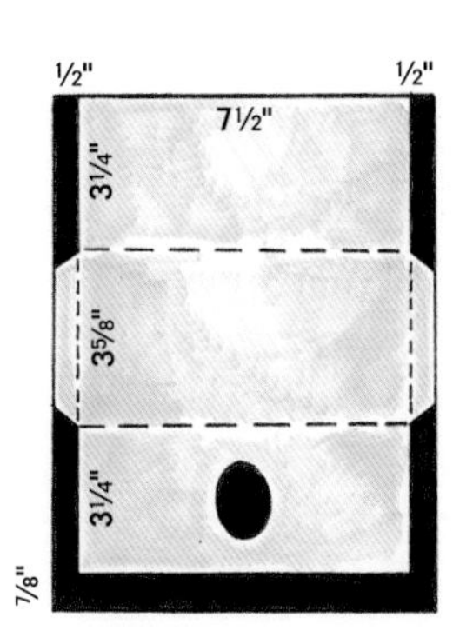

presidential portraits

The portraits in question here are the handsome pocket-size presidential portraits on crisp new paper money! Oval mats display them to perfection, and if you use terrific frames to capture Washington, Lincoln, Jackson, Grant, or Hamilton (though he wasn't a president), your gift will double in value.

Choose a frame that reflects the gift-giving occasion and the taste of the recipient: silver, pewter, wood, or even fabric may be appropriate. Depending on the amount of money you wish to give, pick a single frame, a double frame, or a larger frame with several windows; feel free to mix and match the portraits within a double or larger frame.

what you'll need

- Frame with cardboard backing
- Heavy paper (such as card stock) for the mat
- Tracing paper
- Crisp new bills in the desired denominations
- Manicure or embroidery scissors
- Tape

If the recipient is a design or architecture buff, reverse the bills to frame the Great Seal of the United States, the Lincoln Memorial, the U.S. Treasury Building, the White House, the Capitol, or Independence Hall.

how to do it

1. Open the frame and remove any cardboard backing(s) and glass; discard any ready-made mats.
2. Cut the heavy paper to the same size as the cardboard backing(s).
3. Place the tracing paper over the portrait on the bill and use a pencil to draw an oval that frames the face nicely; you may want to use an artist's oval template (available at art supply stores) to help you draw a perfect shape. Carefully cut out the tracing paper oval.
4. Center the tracing paper oval on each mat, with a bit more space below than above, and trace around it; cut out the traced oval with the scissors.
5. Sandwich the bill between the cardboard backing and the heavy paper mat, positioning the portrait in the oval opening and tape to hold. Fold in the ends of the bill. Put the glass on top of the mat and replace the whole unit in the frame. Close the frame.

MAGIC IN MINUTES

Framing Abe

When you don't have time but you do have a crisp new one-, five-, ten-, twenty-, or fifty-dollar bill, you can still put together a terrific little gift: Buy a small frame, available at art, gift, photo, or drug stores. Neatly fold your crisp bill into a shape small enough to fit into the frame, to display either the portrait, or the picture on the back of the bill.

Vegas Vacation

If the money is intended for a specific purpose, decorate the frame to complement the occasion. Here dice echo the casino theme. Slip the folded bill into the frame—and that's it!

MAGIC IN MINUTES

Extra "Bread"

A loaf of unsliced bread is an amusing double-entendre container for a stack of crisp bills.

Use a sharp serrated knife to slice the bread in half horizontally. From the bottom half, remove a rectangle of bread large enough to accommodate the stack of bills. Put the money in and fit the two halves of the bread together. Tie the bread neatly with raffia, catching a sheaf of wheat in the bow.

For presentation, place the bread on a wooden charger or in a basket. If you're transporting the gift, wrap with cellophane and tie with more raffia.

giving flowers

Flowers give pleasure in so many ways—with their exquisite colors, their diverse textures, their delicious scents. Add a beautiful presentation to the flowers themselves, and you have a gift fit for the most discerning taste. And when the flowers have finally faded, your lucky recipient will still retain a bright, sweet memory of the occasion on which they were given. But there are flowers, and then there are flowers. Lovely as they are, arrangements from the best florist can be extremely costly and may not have as much impact as a simple bouquet from the greenmarket, or from your own yard, in a stylish container.

2

TO BE OVERCOME BY THE FRAGRANCE OF FLOWERS IS A DELECTABLE FORM OF DEFEAT.
—*Beverly Nichols*

A classy copper version of the containers reminiscent of those used by French flower vendors is filled with contemporary terra-cotta Leonardis roses and contrasting hypernicum berries.

For any occasion, nothing is as appropriate and stylish as an armful of blooms straight from the market, placed in one of the simple metal containers reminiscent of those used by French flower vendors. They are available in the authentic galvanized tin, as well as brass-trimmed steel and classy copper.

The impact of your market bouquet will vary according to your choice of flowers and the way you arrange them. Imagine, for instance, filling your metal container with a single variety of flower in a color your recipient loves: lilacs, perhaps, or peachy French tulips. You might choose a glorious array of pastel-colored hydrangeas or snapdragons, a group of zinnias in brilliant colors, or a mixture of anemones, daffodils, and other spring blooms in many varieties. You

This large "bouquet" is actually six little nosegays arranged in one container. Each individual nosegay is tied simply with ribbon so that it's easy to remove from the group.

This presentation makes a charming hostess gift. Or treat your own dinner guests to small favors: Use the arrangement as a centerpiece, and when the party's over, give a nosegay to each guest to take home as a remembrance.

FILLING OUT A BOUQUET

Be creative when you choose materials for filling out your bouquets. Use colorful berries such as bittersweet, eucalyptus baby berries, hypericum, and wildflowers such as salisupra and monte-casino. Consider curly willow, bamboo stakes, or long, graceful bear grass, too. Circling a bouquet or nosegay with galax leaves makes a stunning frame around the blossoms.

Moss is a wonderful finishing touch for many arrangements. Find a source for thick, velvety mood moss; when mood moss is not available, fresh green sheet moss is a fine substitute.

can see how versatile and dramatic these containers can be, and the recipient will surely use the container again.

A gift of flowers need not be expensive. Even wildflowers can make a chic and stylish arrangement—and they're free. Use as many kinds of flowers as you can find—the greater the variety, the more dramatic the arrangement.

FRESH FLOWER TIPS

Wash your container to make sure it's really clean, putting it through the dishwasher if possible. Remember that bacteria can harm fresh flowers.

To aid in arranging the flowers, use chicken wire or frogs at the bottom of any opaque container; if the container is clear, it's preferable to omit the wire or frogs. (Florist's foam [Oasis] is easy to use in flower arrangements and is the choice of many commercial florists, but it does not deliver water very effectively to the stems, so the arrangements may be short-lived.)

1. Fill the container with warm water; use hot water only for flowers with woody stems.

2. Add a splash of bleach to the water to retard the growth of bacteria and prolong flower life.

3. Add sugar, Floralife, or even caffeine-free soft drinks like Sprite to the water, too.

4. Consider using fresh herbs in your arrangement, for texture and aroma. They're particularly nice for arrangements that will go on the dining table.

5. Prepare flowers before arranging them, removing leaves from the lower part of the stems, where they would be submerged in the vase water.

6. Cut the stems at an angle, to allow water to enter the stems. If the stems are cut straight, they'll rest on the bottom of the container and water won't get in.

unusual containers

If you hesitate to give flowers because they seem so ephemeral, consider pairing your floral tribute with a container that has a life beyond its stint as a vase. Many useful and decorative containers can be pressed into service to hold bouquets large or small, and they can add an unexpected touch of whimsy to what might otherwise have been a lovely but predictable gift. They will also continue to remind your loved ones of their special day.

Just keep a few guidelines in mind: Match the scale of your container to the scale of the floral arrangement, and keep your choice appropriate to the flowers themselves; elegant flowers like lilies and roses deserve a refined container, and sprigs of berries and autumn leaves would be nice in something more casual or rustic.

Once you've opened your eyes to the possibilities, you'll want to comb flea markets and housewares departments for interesting new holders for your flowers. Even if you are not arranging the flowers yourself, take a special container to your florist to fill.

SWEET SIPS

This bedside carafe—a pretty vase topped with a drinking glass—allows you to create a pair of flower arrangements. When the flowers are gone, the carafe remains as a thoughtful gift. Accompany this floral presentation with the Japanese proverb, "Happiness is to hold flowers in both hands."

BRUSH-UP BOUQUET

A two-part ceramic toothbrush holder becomes an adorable vase when you tuck flowers into the openings. Condition the flowers (see sidebar page 47), fill the bottom part of the holder with water, and arrange your blooms. The "vase"—available in many styles and colors—may be reused for flowers or even for toothbrushes.

MORNING BLEND

Say "Rise and shine" to a working person, a college student, or any dear friend with this bright, colorful bouquet of tulips, daisies, and daffodils presented in a ceramic latte mug and accompanied by a gift certificate to Starbucks or any other favorite local coffee emporium.

improvising containers

Improvising containers for your floral gifts can make the gift process even more memorable. You can use a "significant container" to hold posies for anyone on your gift list. Choose a holder that will have special meaning. Surprise a childhood friend with whom you shared Ovaltine by using the empty glass jar to hold the flowers. Or select a coffee can for your coffee break buddy at work. Think about the recipient. What container would make the perfect connection? Acknowledge the recipient's passion or recall a shared experience by adding your own special noteworthy sentiments.

FAST AND FUNNY

Gifts given spontaneously can have greater impact than those given to mark an official occasion. Do you know someone who's bearing a heavy load? Lighten it with a gift of flowers arranged in a container that shows you understand her burden—for example, the laundry detergent container shown here, for a hardworking mom. It will be a unique presentation, a special thought from you.

BLACKBOARD JUNGLE

A flared-top terra-cotta vase is a perfect shape for a lush arrangement of tropical flowers. To turn the vase into a writing surface for your special message, paint the container with blackboard paint, following the directions on the can. Include chalk and an eraser with your gift.

UNCANNY FLEURS

When choosing the cans for this presentation, think about which ones would be meaningful to the recipient. Does she love tomatoes? Peaches? Cocoa? Clean the cans carefully, leaving the labels intact. Fill with flowers.

fabulous fakes

Don't limit yourself to what looks fresh at the market. There are many valid reasons to choose artificial flowers: You might be mailing your gift, you might want it to last for a very long time, or you might be giving it to a person who has allergies! Fortunately, the quality of silk flowers has improved tremendously, and it's no longer difficult to select truly gorgeous stems for an arrangement.

Silk roses, for instance, may easily be mistaken for the real thing from a distance. To enhance the realistic appearance of your bouquet, choose roses in several stages, from buds to full blown. Silk gerbera daisies, lilies of the valley, poppies, and lilacs are also favorites.

It's a good idea to use an opaque container for your silk flower arrangement, to conceal the stems and to downplay the obvious fact that these flowers need no water.

OPPOSITE. For even more realism, tear a few petals from one of the flowers and drop them beside the vase as if real petals had fallen. BELOW. Instead of flowers, offer a gourmand a handsome container chock full of flavorful asparagus and watch her eyes light up. Any simple, clear vase with low, straight sides will show off the plump green stalks. Add a pretty cord or ribbon, and you've got a perfectly delicious gift.

flowers, fruits, or vegetables

Gift bouquets needn't be restricted to floral arrangements. Beautiful fruits and vegetables can be used to create interesting and unexpected decorative arrangements. As a matter of fact, there are times when flowers may not be the best choice; strongly fragranced flowers may compete with the aroma of food on the dining table. If the selection at your florist is not as fresh or as special as you had hoped for, or perhaps your florist is closed, that's the time to be really creative. Why not arrange a glorious collection of fresh garden vegetables (see page 64) to be used as a centerpiece, or to brighten the kitchen counter? You could choose succulent fruit to pile on a wicker tray; or you could create a long-lasting topiary of grapes like the one photographed on page 61.

Even if you are convinced that flowers are essential to a bouquet, consider mixing fragrant berries or fresh fruits and vegetables with flowering blossoms to create a unique presentation.

daisy basket

Picture the morning sunlight streaming through this delightful basket of glowing white daisies and forsythia. What could be more charming for a baptism, a sweet sixteen party, or to celebrate the first day of spring?

what you'll need

- Branches of real or silk forsythia (The forsythia in the photograph is silk.)
- Thin wire
- Shallow basket with a handle, and plastic liner to fit
- Block of Oasis (florist's foam)
- Fresh daisies

how to do it

1. Wire the branches of forsythia to the basket handle, using the photograph as a guide.
2. Cut the Oasis to fit in the plastic liner, soak it in water treated with floral preservative, and place it in the liner. Put the liner in the basket.
3. Arrange the daisies in the basket in a generous bouquet, pushing their stems firmly into the Oasis.

Noteworthy Sentiments

"JUST LIVING IS NOT ENOUGH SAID THE BUTTERFLY. ONE MUST HAVE SUNSHINE, FREEDOM, AND A LITTLE FLOWER."

—*Hans Christian Andersen*

spring garden

Even if you can't remember to force bulbs in the spring, you can make this wonderful presentation of tulips, daffodils, and hyacinths, and it will look just like a miniature spring garden supported by a bamboo fence.

what you'll need

- 6 bamboo stakes, each 12″ long
- Raffia
- Green moss
- Block of Oasis (florist's foam)
- Basket and plastic liner to fit
- Spring flowers that grow from bulbs, such as tulips, daffodils, hyacinths, narcissus, and freesia

how to do it

1. To make the bamboo fence, first overlap three stakes to form a triangle; lash together with raffia. Add a vertical stake at each corner, and lash securely with raffia. If you like, trim each intersection with a bit of green moss.
2. Cut the Oasis to fit in the plastic liner, soak it in water treated with floral preservative, and place it in the liner. Put the liner in the basket.
3. Sink the three legs of the bamboo fence firmly into the Oasis. Arrange the spring flowers in clumps—a cluster of tulips, a few hyacinths, and so on—pushing their stems into the Oasis. Cover any exposed Oasis with green moss.

Noteworthy Sentiments

To celebrate spring, or just because:

THE EARTH LAUGHS IN FLOWERS.

—*Ralph Waldo Emerson*

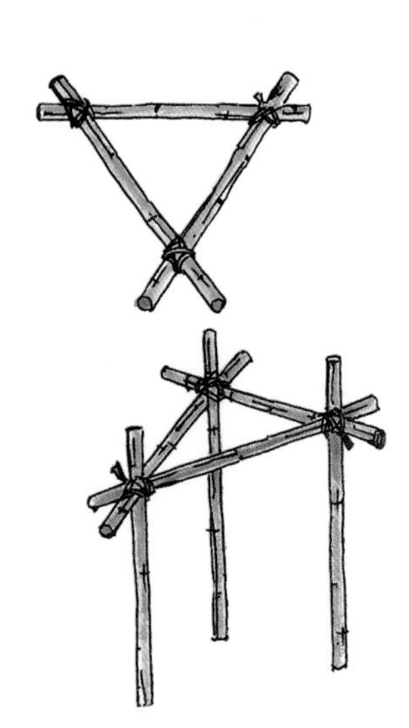

carnation topiary

Carnations deserve more respect than they usually receive. Their virtues are many: They are readily available, reasonably priced, long-lasting, sweet-smelling, and pretty. This elegant topiary presentation, which can last up to two weeks, does them justice. Roses, sunflowers, or amaryllis work well too.

what you'll need

- Block of Oasis (florist's foam)
- 7″ terra-cotta azalea pot and plastic liner to fit
- 12 to 18 carnations
- 12 galax leaves
- Thin wire
- Green sheet moss
- 5 yards of 1½″-wide wire-edged ribbon

how to do it

1. Cut the Oasis to fit in the plastic liner, soak it in water treated with floral preservative, and place it in the liner. Put the liner in the terra-cotta pot.
2. To create the topiary, begin by holding one carnation, which will be the center top, and then add one stem at a time around the center. Keep adding carnations and galax leaves to create a round, even ball. Grip the stems tightly at the base of the ball and secure with wire.
3. Cut the stems, if needed, and push them deep into the Oasis. Tear a circle of moss slightly larger than the pot. Tear the circle from the edge to the center, and wrap it around the stems to cover the Oasis.
4. Cut a 2-yard length of ribbon and fold it to narrow the width. Find the center of the piece and begin at the base of the stems, wrapping, criss-crossing, and twisting the ribbon as you work up the stems. Knot the ribbon at the base of the ball.
5. With the remaining 3 yards of ribbon, make a florist's bow, following the directions on page 111. Tie the bow to the top of the stems.

Noteworthy Sentiments

To express condolences or support:

WHEN WORDS ESCAPE, FLOWERS SPEAK.

—*Robert Currie*

grape topiary

The grapes are fake, but the look is convincing—and terrific. The topiary in the photograph required about 350 grapes.

what you'll need

- Block of Sahara (Styrofoam)
- Heavy pot or container, about 6″ in diameter (If you use a lightweight container, you'll need plaster instead of Sahara to anchor the trunk of the topiary and keep the container from toppling.)
- Straight tree branch, 18″ to 20″ long
- 4″-diameter Styrofoam ball
- Hot glue gun and glue sticks
- Several bunches of artificial grapes
- Ball-headed straight pins
- Green sheet moss

how to do it

1. Cut the foam to fit inside the container and place it inside. Insert the tree branch in the foam to make the trunk of the topiary. (If you are using a lightweight container, fill with plaster of paris, place the branch in the plaster, and allow to set.)
2. Press the Styrofoam ball down on top of the trunk to create a channel. Remove the ball, put hot glue on the trunk, and glue the ball in place.
3. Remove individual grapes from the bunches. Hot-glue a ball-headed pin into the opening of each grape.
4. Beginning at the top, pin grapes to the ball, with grapes touching one another, creating an all-over pattern. Add smaller grapes to fill in between larger ones so the ball is completely covered.
5. Conceal the foam (or plaster) with moss. If you like, glue bits of moss to the trunk.

If you choose to create an edible centerpiece, adapt the directions at right. Choose a 4–5-inch diameter Styrofoam ball and glue it securely at the top of the branch so that it will not shift when handled. You may prepare the base ahead of schedule, but the freshly washed grapes should be added just before serving. Use toothpicks with points on both ends; skewer a grape on one end, and push the other end into the Styrofoam ball, arranging the grapes to cover the sphere completely. You may want to use a variety of grapes for added color, texture, and flavor.

MAGIC IN MINUTES

Floating Flower

To fully appreciate a beautiful fragrant gardenia, simply float it in a shallow bowl filled with water. A bloom this perfect needs nothing else to complement it.

For a gift presentation, choose a bowl appropriate to the taste and lifestyle of the recipient: silver, Thai glass, ceramic, fine china, or something attractive (but inexpensive) from an import store.

Of course, this idea will work with any number of other flowers, too. Choose an uneven number of blossom heads—one, three, or five—from classic roses to colorful gerbera daisies, or elegant orchids.

MAGIC IN MINUTES

A Single Tulip

For this chic tulip presentation, begin with a small terra-cotta pot painted matte black, and use adhesive mounting putty (such as Fun Tak) to secure a frog in the bottom. Add water. Carefully remove a leaf from the tulip, trim the stem to 6 inches, then insert the tulip stem into the frog. Now wrap the leaf around the base of the tulip, letting it extend over the side of the pot.

giving food

There's nothing more caring than a gift of food, especially if it's a favorite food presented in a delicious and tantalizing way. And with food preparation time at a premium in most households, sharing good things to eat with family and friends is a welcome act of kindness. You need not be a chef or a baker to make a gift of food. In this chapter you'll find everything from fresh herbs to junk food, and not one of them requires cooking or preparation. Your gifts of food will leave your loved ones with happy taste buds, and the sensational presentations will turn your gifts into truly special memories.

FOOD IS OUR COMMON GROUND, A UNIVERSAL EXPERIENCE.
—*James Beard*

Fresh vegetables make thoughtful, healthy gifts for any occasion, or "just because." No time to garden? In season, shop your local farmer's market for a beautiful array of veggies to arrange in a deep gardening basket. Complete your gift presentation by adding gardening gloves, tools, or packets of seeds.

gift baskets

Personalize your gifts of food so that they won't appear to be generic food baskets. Create an experience for eating; carefully choose the ingredients for your gift so that they are specific to the recipient, and then select a special container to hold the collection. A well-chosen container can be reused or recycled and enhances the value of your gift. You may choose to assemble ingredients for cooking a specific meal to be wrapped in a pot, bowl, or wok. Or you could assemble a ready-to-eat meal in a picnic basket or lunch box, or use a gardening basket for fresh vegetables, or why not use a small reusable garbage pail for an abundant stash of nibbles?

Fill a natural rattan picnic basket with the Sunday paper; a chilled split of champagne and some orange juice for mimosas; steaming hot coffee in a thermos; the best croissants you can find; yummy preserves and sweet butter; fresh fruit; champagne flutes, plates, cups, flatware, and cloth napkins. Top the basket with a Do Not Disturb sign.

And don't forget: If the recipient isn't a champagne-and-croissant type, bagels, lox, and cream cheese are just as good. So are paper napkins and plates—and they're easy to dispose of when brunch is over.

A little planning will go a long way toward making this a successful gift presentation: You'll want to call ahead to be sure the recipient will be home and available to enjoy your generosity.

DO
NOT
DISTURB

THE PBJ BASKET

Choose a very special basket for this gift presentation, and fill it with perennial favorites: peanut butter, jars of jelly and jam, great bread, and lots of peanuts in the shell. If you like, go for an even jazzier assortment: jars of gourmet preserves, organic peanut butter or almond butter, home-baked bread, fancy crackers. Or substitute packages of scones and lemon curd for the bread and peanut butter.

To dress up the jars, cut rounds from kraft paper; the diameter of each round should be 3″ greater than the diameter of the lid it will cover. Secure with raffia.

HERBS

Fresh herbs are fragrant, earthy, and unparalleled for cooking. On top of all that, they make great arrangements for the kitchen or dining area. Be sure to include a few recipes that use fresh herbs to advantage.

Recipe Extravaganza

Cooks—aspiring or experienced—will love these gifts and adore the presentation. Do a little detective work, or just keep your ears wide open for clues, to discover your friend's favorite recipe. It might be for a dish she's eaten and loved at your house, or it might be something she's found in a cookbook, or a traditional family recipe or even a restaurant recipe. Surprise her with all the exotic or hard-to-get ingredients, plus some of the necessary equipment and, of course, the recipe neatly written out. Pack it all in an appropriate container, add decorations, wrap in cellophane—and she'll be able to prepare that dish any time she chooses.

TASTE OF ASIA

This gift is for a friend who can't get enough hoisin chicken. Start with a favorite recipe tucked into a traditional red envelope. Select the special ingredients—hoisin sauce, sesame oil, rice noodles, tapioca, Chinese tea, a wire strainer, a sieve, chopsticks, and a Chinese fan for decoration—and assemble it all in a shiny new wok. To present your gift, wrap in cellophane and tie with a vivid cord.

SELF-STICK LETTERS

Applying self-stick letters is easy if you plan ahead and take your time. Be sure to plan out your design *before* you remove any letters from the backing, because once you place the letters, they can't be easily moved.

Write your message on paper to figure out the number of lines it will require. Draw two parallel lines for each line of letters, to insure correct placement.

Count the number of letters needed, and estimate how much space they'll take up. You'll then be able to plan your message so that it follows your design, centering the lines if necessary. Working from the center of each line to the left and right helps to achieve the most accurate placement. Peel the letters from the backing one at a time and apply them to the tag, package, or box. Once the placement is correct, rub the letters firmly to adhere them.

scoop of nuts

Most folks just can't get enough pistachios, so a hefty scoopful is a welcome gift. A No. 1 scoop like this one holds about 2¼ cups of pistachios in the shell.

For the presentation, fold a 17" square of cellophane in half. Fill the scoop with pistachios (or any desired nuts) and slide the scoop into the folded cellophane all the way to the fold; be sure the scoop is centered in the cellophane. Gather the cellophane at the neck of the scoop and tie tightly with raffia.

what you'll need

- Card stock
- Silver marker
- Pressure-sensitive stick-on vinyl letters
- Reinforcement ring
- Raffia

how to do it

1. Cut a tag out of the card stock.
2. With the silver marker, draw a line ⅛" from the edge of the tag.
3. Plan your message on a piece of scrap paper, and then make guidelines on the tag so you can correctly place the letters according to your plan design.
4. Glue the reinforcement ring to the narrow end of the tag, and make a hole through the center.
5. Double the piece of raffia, push the looped end through the hole, and slip the loose ends through the loop. Pull tight and tie to the handle of the scoop.

Noteworthy Sentiments

For a special someone:

HERE'S THE SCOOP—

I'M NUTTY ABOUT YOU!

TO
UNCLE
JOHN
XOXO

REMOVING A STICKY LABEL

Removing price tags and labels from hard surfaces can be frustrating work. Try these tips:

- Use a hair dryer to soften the adhesive before you try to peel the label off.
- Single-edge razor blades can be helpful in scraping off labels, but only if surfaces won't be harmed.
- Goo Gone removes any adhesive left on the surface after a label is peeled off. Test it on a small area first to make sure it doesn't mar the color or finish of the gift or wrap.
- Nail polish remover takes away the sticky stuff from glass; on other surfaces, test first.
- Undo adhesive remover won't damage surfaces; it removes stickers, tape, labels, gum, and so on.

very private label

This is a fabulous birthday gift for a gourmand, for the man who has everything, or for anyone who'd be thrilled and flattered by a completely custom-designed presentation. The wine itself can be as good as you like, but it's the custom label on the bottle that makes the gift. Name the "vineyard" after the recipient, declare him "aged to perfection for sixty years" (or thirty, forty, or fifty years), describe him in wine terminology—light, crisp, full of body, and so on. Celebrate his accomplishments right there on the label.

To duplicate this presentation, soak the labels off a purchased bottle of wine. Create your own labels by computer (using a label template or other software), by hand, or by designing them and having them made up by your local printer. Put an illustration on the front label; it might be a child's drawing or a color copy of a family photo. Use double-face tape or glue to attach the new label to the wine bottle.

See page 107 in Part 5 for an elegant wrapping for your gift.

all-american junk food

They used to say "Send a salami to your boy in the army," but nowadays your kids in the service or at camp or college would probably prefer a rescue package of good old American junk food. A garbage can makes a fitting receptacle for a cache of "junk." If it includes some of Mom's home-baked cookies or Dad's famous carrot bread, so much the better.

what you'll need

- Pressure-sensitive stick-on vinyl letters
- A 10-gallon galvanized garbage can
- Card stock or a blank tag, silver paper, glue, and press-on letters, for the tag
- Ball-chain key ring
- Assorted junk food, to fill the can completely

how to do it

1. Position the stick-on vinyl letters in the channels of the garbage can to spell "Junk Food"; 3″-high condensed letters will fit perfectly into the channels of the garbage can. (See page 70 for hints on working with stick-on letters.)
2. From card stock, cut a tag and glue silver paper to the face of the tag. Decide what your message will be, and apply press-on letters to spell it out, or if you prefer, hand-letter the message.
3. Punch a hole in the end of the tag. Slip one end of the ball-chain through the hole and then through the handle of the garbage can lid; fasten the chain.
4. Stuff the garbage can with packages of junk food, fit the lid in place, and secure.

Noteworthy Sentiments

THERE IS NO LOVE SINCERER THAN THE LOVE OF FOOD.

—*George Bernard Shaw*

TOO MUCH
OF A GOOD THING
IS WONDERFUL
ENJOY
Hostess
Twinkies
12
13

MAGIC IN MINUTES

Nothing Chocolate, Nothing Gained

No gift wrap? No ribbon? No problem! Wrap a box of chocolates in a smoothed-out brown paper bag, then cut words and letters from magazines and catalogs to spell out your message.

taste test

To a food maven, few things are more gratifying than tasting, tasting, tasting. We all know people who are constantly searching for the best example of a favorite taste sensation. Give your gourmet the ultimate pleasure: a gift of taste testing. Gourmets pride themselves on knowing what's available, and they certainly can describe the taste experience in minute detail. Collect six or more samples of any favorite food or beverage—chocolate chip cookies, sourdough bread, beer, salsa, potato chips, goat cheese, olive oil, coffee, tea—and package them up nicely. Use a lined basket to cradle olive rolls or a galvanized bucket of ice to hold a sampling of flavored beers. And to enhance your gift idea, create a scorecard to accompany your presentation.

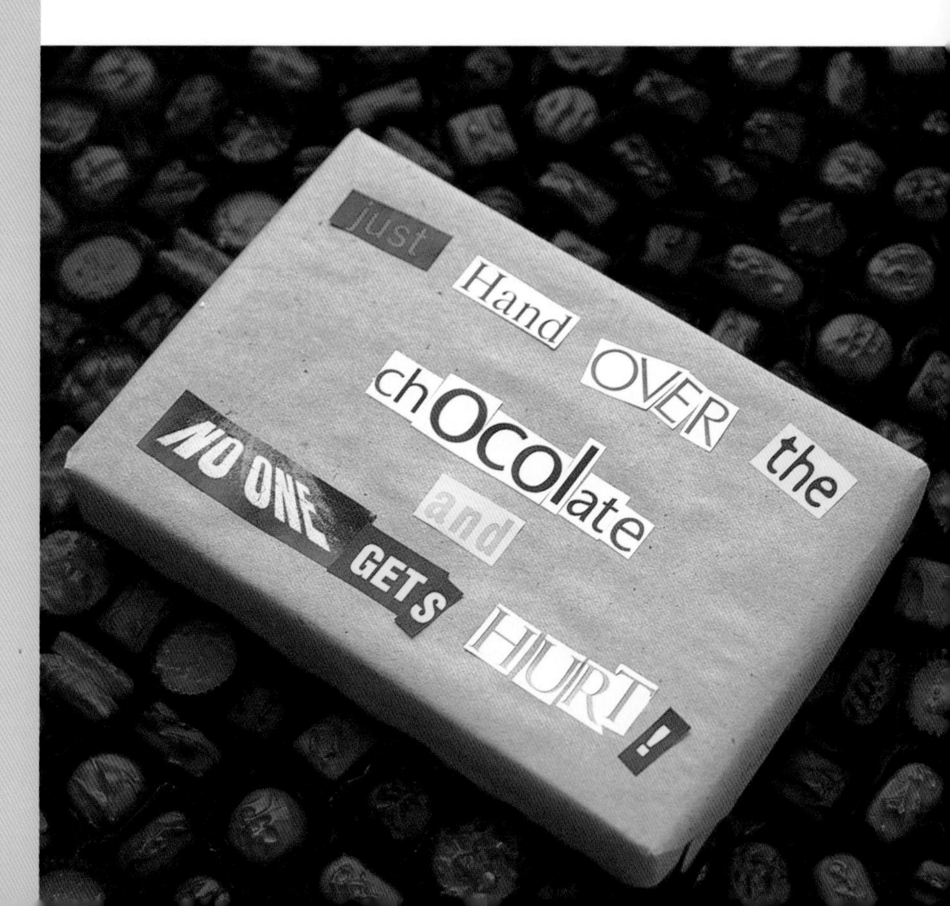

MAGIC IN MINUTES

Luscious Olives

Olives are an ideal food gift because they come in so many varieties, they need not be refrigerated—and they're so delicious! Simply fill a beautiful bowl with olives—either a single kind or a pick-and-choose selection—and add a pretty olive pick and perhaps a packet of paper napkins.

giving other gifts

This chapter covers gifts that offer wonderful experiences to the recipients—small, quiet experiences such as reading good books or relaxing in a luxurious bath; enriching experiences such as attending lectures or concerts; exciting experiences such as taking trips. By thinking carefully about what would be truly special to your friends and relatives, you'll come up with a gift that will be cherished forever in memory. Enhance the impact of your present with clever packaging, to make the most of the present.

GIVING PRESENTS IS A TALENT; TO KNOW WHAT A PERSON WANTS, TO KNOW WHEN AND HOW TO GIVE IT, TO GIVE IT LOVINGLY AND WELL. UNLESS A CHARACTER POSSESSES THIS TALENT THERE IS NO MOMENT MORE ANNIHILATING TO EASE THAN THAT IN WHICH A PRESENT IS RECEIVED AND GIVEN.

—*Pamela Gleneoumer*

GIFTS THAT COUNT

For the friends and relatives who possess all the material things they need, consider making a donation to a worthy charity, from God's Love We Deliver or the Make-A-Wish Foundation to Heifer Project International, which offers goats, rabbits, or honeybees to needy families around the world. Be creative when announcing your gift donation: For a gift of honeybees, accompany the gift card supplied by the organization with a jar of honey topped with a honeybee tie-on.

There is a multitude of interesting and unusual ways to present these gifts, too. If you thumb through this part of the book, you'll see that the gifts vary in expense, so you can make your gift as simple or as extravagant as you like. A gift of time, such as a daily phone call costing almost nothing, can be the most precious gift of all to a person who is sad or lonely. A gift of sentiment —a poem or loving message—can be a treasure as valuable as a string of pearls. And conversely, to someone on a tight budget, the gift of a museum membership or a stack of new CDs will bring joy for many months.

Sometimes a traditional gift *is* the perfect choice, especially for someone you don't know well. But you need not make your presentation standard issue.

ZAGAT
NEW YORK CITY RESTAURANTS

CANDLES

Candles can be a wonderful gift if they're the right kind: elegant, in beautiful colors, even scented if the fragrance is subtle and classy. (In other words, beware of strong-smelling candles in wild colors!)

There are many candle options: tiny votives appropriate for a bathroom or bedroom; beeswax tapers; a collection of chubby candles of varying heights to decorate a mantelpiece; graceful white, cream, or pastel tapers for the dining room; tall pillar candles to place inside an unlit fireplace. You can even create your own candles, using wax and wicks from a craft store.

HANGERS

A good hanger—whether it's made of wood, padded fabric, tubular metal, or sturdy plastic—is an asset to any closet. A set of matching hangers to replace those flimsy wire ones from the dry cleaner is a thoughtful gift for hosts, newlyweds, or a housewarming. Line up the hangers and secure the necks with a rubber band. Center the group of hangers diagonally on a 40″ square of cellophane. Fill the central space with cedar balls, sachets, or closet potpourri. Gather the cellophane at the necks of the hangers and tie with raffia.

TOILETRIES

Handmade and other fancy soaps make lovely tokens of thanks for hostesses, teachers, helpers, and friends. To individualize your gift and show you've given time and thought to what could be a ho-hum item, wrap soaps with unusual paper tied with slender wire and top them with small semiprecious stones or crystals. Your choice of stones may be based on the recipient's birthstone (see page 124) or simply how it looks with the wrapping paper.

BOOKS FOR ALL

Books make splendid gifts and there is definitely a book to suit everyone on your list. Select books relating to the special interests of the recipient: books on sports or hobbies, on gardening or interiors, humor books, mysteries, a travel book—the possibilities are endless.

For a wine connoisseur, present a fine bottle of wine with a book on wine. Wrap in corrugated paper, punch two holes through all on that carries out the theme, layers at each end, and tie with cord to close. The finishing touch? Wine bottle corks threaded onto the cord ends.

giving great experiences

Shifting the gift-giving process from just choosing things, to sharing experiences and opportunities, will change your perspective and make the art of giving a true gift. Now, more than ever, it IS the thought that counts. The next time you select a gift, instead of picking out an object or an item of clothing, give your loved one a memorable experience that you present in an unforgettable way. Make your selection based on what he or she likes to do . . . travel, pamper himself, attend a concert or play, learn a new sport, or just relax at home with dinner and a movie. The following presentations are just a few of the myriad ways you can dress up your gift to delight friends and family.

Noteworthy Sentiments

For an anniversary:

IT'S TEE FORE TWO!

For a birthday:

TWENTY-NINE (OR PERSON'S AGE) SUITS YOU TO A TEE.

This is a lively presentation for a gift of paid-up time on the golf course for your favorite golf aficionado. To re-create it, you'll need a shallow glass bowl (the one photographed is five inches in diameter and three inches high), some soil, rye grass seeds, a golf tee and ball, a bit of adhesive putty, and a gift certificate or scorecard from the golf course.

A week before presenting the gift, plant the seeds in 2½ inches of soil in the bowl; mist the grass each day. On the day of presentation, trim the grass evenly about 3½ inches above the edge of the bowl. Insert the tee and attach the golf ball with the putty. Include the gift certificate or a scorecard on which to explain the gift. To make this a last-minute gift, skip the grass-growing step and purchase a square of sod and cut it to fit the glass bowl.

Staff
TITANIUM
4
Upper Montclair

THE TICKET EXPERIENCE

Tickets to a concert of classical, rock, or jazz music; to the opera, a play, or a musical; to a dance performance, a sporting event, or a magic show; to a film festival or Shakespeare under the stars—these experiences are yours for the giving. Make your gift more than just a ticket in an envelope by presenting it in a special way. For example, package concert tickets with a pretty Lucite piano, tucking the tickets into a card with your message written inside.

THE RELAXATION EXPERIENCE

Pamper a good (and busy) friend with this luxe basket of products that encourage relaxation. Color-coordinate the items you choose for maximum visual impact, and top the collection with a bouquet of lavender tied with a beautiful ribbon.

Select some or all of the following possibilities: towel and washcloth; eye pad; candle; tub teabags; buckwheat hull or tub pillow; split of champagne and champagne flute; bath salts; relaxing book; CD of calming music—*but* be wary of mixing too many fragrances in this gift.

DINNER AND A MOVIE

Some busy folks never take time out for dinner and a movie, but you can give them a homestyle version of a night on the town. No special occasion is necessary, but do plan it for a day and hour that you're certain will be convenient for the recipient. Stack up a frozen dinner, video, and popcorn, and secure them in position with bits of adhesive putty. Loosely tie a film strip around the stack and use press-on letters to write your message.

THE TRIP EXPERIENCE

Giving a trip—a flight of fancy—can mean anything from a weekend at a cozy bed-and-breakfast to a week in Rome. Arrange to pay for the trip without booking a specific date, especially for anything nonrefundable. For some trips it's possible to give prepaid reservations with no precise date attached, or to book reservations very far in advance so the recipient can alter them.

To present your gift, collect brochures, an empty ticket folder, and travel guides and package them with a note explaining the trip.

GIFT
of the
MONTH

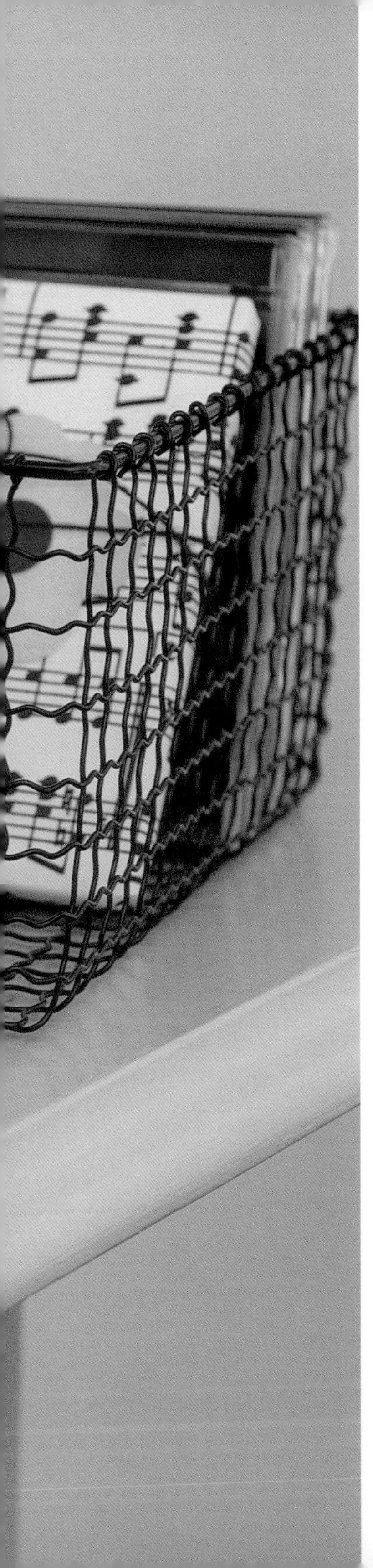

gift of the month

A gift that arrives regularly once a month for a year is a treat twelve times over! Decide on your gift according to what the recipient really enjoys and what you can afford. And don't limit your thinking to prepackaged mail order options; select, wrap, and deliver each month's treat yourself!

Ideas include a monthly presentation of a new compact disk, with the first CD arriving in a wire CD basket large enough to hold at least eleven more. Use the same wrapping paper for each month's offering, and add a seasonal tag.

Here are some other possibilities for gifts of the month:

- Beer or wine
- Flowers presented in a beautiful vase, with the vase to be reused each month
- Movie tickets or video rentals
- Soaps or candles
- Candy or chocolates
- Books
- Recipes
- Poems
- An assortment of gifts relating to one theme, such as angels, baseball, a color, or a country
- A voucher good for a service, such as baby-sitting or shopping

To make the seasonal tags, cut simple shapes from bright-colored card stock; the photograph shows a few appropriate shapes, and you'll come up with a few of your own, too. Cut a slit in each tag, and slide it onto the cord with which you've tied your package.

i miss you gift

Although this gift was invented for a traveling dad to leave with his little girl, you may adapt it for any number of "I miss you" occasions. Each compartment is just right for holding tiny toys; chocolate truffles; office trinkets, such as paper clips, pushpins, or erasers; love notes; recipes; poems; jokes; and even priceless jewels.

what you'll need

- Seven-day pill container box
- $8\frac{1}{2}$″ × 11″ sheet of paper for card
- 8″ × 10″ piece of tissue paper for each compartment
- Collection of small treats

how to do it

1. To create the card on your computer, use the landscape orientation and a keystroke font. Alternatively letter by hand.
2. Divide an $8\frac{1}{2}$″ × 11″ piece of paper lengthwise into four sections: three sections, each $2\frac{3}{8}$″ wide, and one remaining section $1\frac{7}{8}$″ wide, which will be cut off and discarded later.
3. In the first section, center letters *A* through *M* and letters *N* through *Z*, omitting the letter *U*, but leaving the letter space blank.
4. Leave the second section blank, for writing your personal note; in the third section, enter the message, "I MISS U."
5. Print out the page, cut off the $1\frac{7}{8}$″-wide section, and fold as shown.
6. Wrap each gift separately in tissue paper, and nest in its own compartment.

C D E F G H I J K L M
P Q R S T V W X Y
THURSDAY
FRIDAY
W T F S

DEAR JANICE,
HAPPY 60TH!
LA TOUR EIFFEL
L'avancement des travaux 1888-1889

celebratory signatures

Here's a keepsake that money can't buy, an extremely personal gift that requires the participation of many friends and relatives. It will take time, effort, and a certain amount of organization to make this gift presentation.

In form, it's simple: a large poster covered with handwritten good wishes and messages of love for the recipient. The occasion may be a marker birthday such as the fiftieth or sixtieth, an anniversary, a wedding, or a graduation. The poster may relate to any part of the recipient's life—a picture of a favorite place, a favorite painting, a favorite musician, and so on. In the photograph, the poster shows the Eiffel Tower, and it commemorates a sixtieth-birthday trip to Paris; the givers carried the poster to Paris and presented it at the Eiffel Tower.

what you'll need

- Large poster or picture
- Letter to request participation
- Avery clear labels, 1″ × 2⅝″
- Mailing list of friends, relatives, co-workers
- Stamped, self-addressed envelopes

how to do it

1. Well before the date of presentation, choose the poster for the recipient and prepare a letter that requests each participant to sign a label in black ink and mail it back to you as soon as possible. Include a few extra labels to allow for practice, and a stamped, self-addressed envelope.
2. When all the signed labels have been returned to you, lay them out on the poster to plan your arrangement. Balance the design, distributing different writing styles across the poster.
3. Peel off the backing of each label and press it in position. Don't forget to add your own personal message.
4. Roll the poster around a cardboard tube. Wrap the tube in appropriate paper, then in cellophane. Tie the top and bottom with single bows. Make a larger bow, following the instructions on page 111, and attach it near the top of the tube, adding any tie-ons you like.

MAGIC IN MINUTES

Seeing Double

Do you have a friend who's constantly searching for her reading glasses? Make life easier with the gift of a stylish chain for her to hang around her neck. The gift will be amusing and memorable if you attach the chain to a pair of novelty glasses. The minute she opens the package, she'll know what the chain is for. Or, if new reading glasses would be a welcomed gift, select a stack of paperbacks for a good read at the beach and top the package with a pair of inexpensive reading glasses or sun readers to cut the glare and magnify the type.

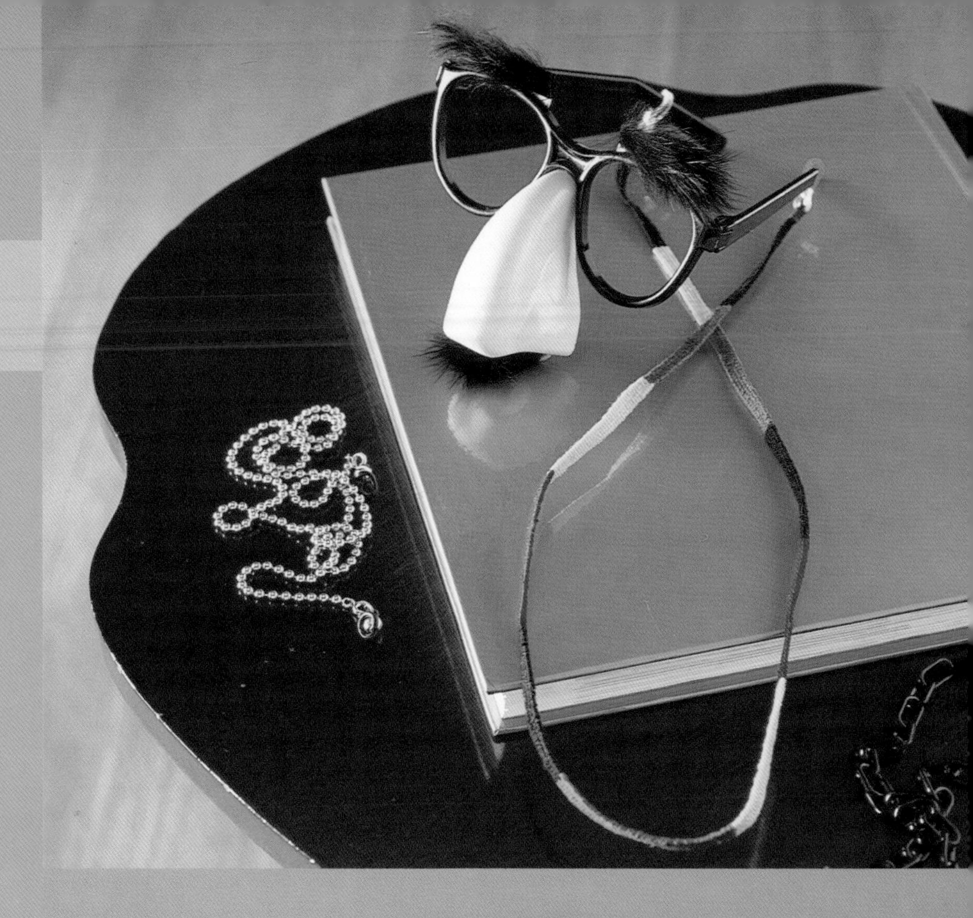

beware of collectibles

Some people are charmed by gifts of their favorite collectibles . . . but not everyone is. Part of the enjoyment in collecting a particular object or motif is the search and discovery by the collector.

In Chinese astrology, I am a snake, so of course I have a few prized specimens. But part of the reason I value them is that they remind me of the trips on which I found them, or in some cases, the artist who carved them. Collectors tend to guard their collectibles preference so that they are not gifted to death with unattractive, ill-designed, and just plain ugly interpretations of something they love. So choose wisely and well. Make certain your contribution to another's collection will indeed be a much appreciated gift.

You can, however, safely acknowledge a person's interest by choosing a related card or package decoration that is disposable, if not adored.

MAGIC IN MINUTES

Car Wash

Here's a presentation for a car-related gift, small or large.

- Tuck car-wash coupons between a toy car and a bar of soap and tie together with ribbon or cord.
- Top a triple-A membership and all the AAA literature with a toy car and tie together with ribbon or cord.
- Knot a ribbon or cord around a toy car and, before you tie the bow, add the keys to a new car!

to Todd

wrapping and other presentations

5

Where gifts are concerned, never underestimate the importance of the presentation. The more gorgeously or cleverly a gift is packaged, the happier anyone will be to receive it!

In this chapter, you'll find handy lists of essentials for gift wrapping, instructions on how to wrap boxes and tie bows, suggestions for unusual containers, strategies for wrapping oversize gifts, and ideas for embellishing packages with interesting add-ons. You'll also find suggestions for organizing your wrapping supplies so you can be efficient.

THE MANNER OF GIVING IS WORTH MORE THAN THE GIFT.

—Pierre Corneille, 1643

This stunning collection of wrapped gifts was created using the contents of a well-stocked gift-wrap pantry. A variety of stylish papers were tied with elegant ribbons and embellished with interesting decorative tie-ons, from understated preserved leaves, to silken blossoms and trailing ivy, to pearly grapes and a lush wreath sprinkled with blooms.

being prepared

When it comes to wrapping gifts, being prepared is more than half the battle. Dashing out for last-minute supplies can be a costly add on that puts a gift overbudget, and it is stressful—hardly a good way to get your creative juices flowing.

To devise truly inspired wrappings you must have (a) a clear space in which to work, preferably an area devoted to nothing else; (b) time to experiment with different materials and effects; and (c) a well-stocked pantry of wrapping materials. Start with the basics (see Gift Wrap Essentials) and gradually accumulate additional supplies over time. Lastly, devise a system for keeping track of your finds, and keeping them readily accessible.

No matter what your budget, you will find fabulous fun options for making your gift even more special. Whether you recycle a plain brown paper bag or invest in an expensive container or wrapping paper, your gifts will always be the stars at the party if you incorporate a few fresh new concepts into your repertoire. Read on . . . I promise you will have fun.

Explore wrapping ideas to keep people guessing about the contents of your presents. Use a prosaic necktie box to conceal opera or sporting event tickets. Wrap a tiny gift in the largest box you can find. Or wrap a collection of small items in crepe paper streamers to form a ball, changing paper color as you add each small gift. Such tricks make the opening of a present as exciting as what's inside.

- Instead of using theme paper, customize plain paper for specific occasions with special tie-ons, ribbons, and cards.
- A corsage bag makes a quick festive wrap when you line the bag with colorful tissue paper and tie it with ribbon or raffia.
- When you store a roll of paper, don't tape the cut edge to the roll; it will damage the paper when you remove the tape. Instead, wrap and tape a small piece of paper around the roll; it will slip off easily next time you want to unroll the wrapping paper.

OPPOSITE. An unusual Japanese paper, a delicate trimming of metallic grosgrain ribbon, and a pair of lacy leaves make this an especially elegant wrapping.

GIFT WRAP ESSENTIALS

With these essentials on hand, you'll always be able to wrap a gift quickly and professionally. You might even assemble the basics in a storage container for a unique gift, *below.*

- Simple wrapping paper in a solid color, either the largest, most cost-effective roll you can find or a paper that becomes your signature, such as white, red, or silver paper
- Double-stick tape
- Paper shears and fabric shears
- Paper punch
- Metallic pens
- Cellophane wrap in 20"- or 40"-wide rolls
- Cellophane bags
- Tissue paper in assorted colors for mixing and matching (If you use a lot of Kraft paper, buy tissue in brown, too.)
- Raffia or twine
- Ribbon
- Measuring tape or ruler

- Save leftover bits of wrapping paper by rolling them up and tucking them into the end of the paper's cardboard tube. The bits are handy for wrapping small gifts or making tags to match the wrap.

Virtually anything can become part of presenting a gift. Just let your ideas flow and consider the incredible possibilities. Imagine the fun of using an empty paint can, paper lantern, steamer basket, or picture frame to house your gift. You'll find dozens of great ideas for innovative presentations.

Presenting gifts has always been fun for me. Creating clever, stunning, or unexpected presentations brings me great satisfaction. I love knowing that my wraps are often recycled, or even rewrapped to sit under the tree, because they are special. Following are some of the tricks I've learned to make giving gifts truly rewarding.

JAMES SIERS
PROVENCE THE BEAUTIFUL COOKBOOK
PAGE ONE
PERIOD DETAILS
Webster's New Collegiate

THE ULTIMATE GIFT WRAP PANTRY

Don't try to acquire this entire list in a single shopping spree; it's a collection to be accumulated over time. Pick up items when you find them. Look for good buys, and stock up at discount stores, garage sales, and end-of-season closeouts. When you see, for example, the perfect tie-on for someone on your gift list, buy it and tuck it away in your Gift Wrap Pantry. When that person's birthday or some other occasion arrives, you'll be glad you have it.

• Wrapping paper: supplement your basic solid with a collection of metallic papers in beautiful colors
• Other assorted papers: art papers, crepe paper, rice paper, handmade papers, marbled paper, corrugated paper
• Special tissue papers: metallic, printed, Mylar
• Fabrics for wrapping large or irregularly shaped gifts: tulle or netting, Indian silks, plain or star-studded organza
• Paper bags in a variety of sizes, finishes (matte and shiny), colors, and metallics
• Special containers: baskets, craft boxes, paper lanterns, empty paint cans, and vases
• Filler materials: excelsior, crinkled filler papers, shredded tissue paper
• Tape, stickers, adhesive labels
• Ribbons in assorted colors, materials, and widths, from shimmering metallics to wired taffetas to solid grosgrains
• Raffia, cords, twine, rattail, wire, wire garlands of stars, snowflakes, or hearts
• Confetti: basic multicolor paper, as well as novelty designs (musical theme, birthday theme, stars) for sprinkling inside packages or cards
• Tie-on package ornaments for decorating your wraps: cookie cutters, silk flowers, fruit, vegetables, birds and nests, lollipops, twigs and sprigs of greenery, holiday ornaments, seashells, preserved leaves, spools of thread, special pencils, small toys, and bells
• Markers and pens: assorted colors and metallics for decorating packages and writing tags and cards
• Decorative paper punches, available in a variety of shapes such as stars, hearts, and flowers
• Embossing stylus, stencils, rubber stamps for embossing and decorating wrappings, cards, and tags

Building a Card Stash

Collecting special cards can be a real time-saver in the long run. When you see the perfect card for someone, buy it. It may be a birthday card and the date is eleven months away, but chances are you won't be able to find one as perfect when the date rolls around. I purchase some of my favorite cards at airport shops while waiting to board, so my stash grows with each flight!

Buy cards and tags whenever you find them—scout drugstores, paper stores, and gift stores. And think *variety:* plain, fancy, pretty, funny, old-fashioned, contemporary, in all sizes, shapes, colors, and themes. Be sure to have plenty with blank interiors.

Designate a specific place for storing your cards so that when the time comes, you can easily find the one you want. Shoe boxes are an ideal size. They're sturdy and you can identify the contents in the frame on the end of the box.

Sometimes you can purchase an ideal card, but often a custom card that you create is the best way to personalize your gift. Find a photo that is relevant, or clip one from a magazine or catalog (use it as is, or color-copy it to adjust the size for your needs), or simply cut out festive shapes. (The "noteworthy sentiments" scattered throughout the book may be helpful in writing the message for your gift card.)

Embossing is a fast and effective technique for creating custom cards that look professional. Metal stencils are available for letters, as well as more designs than you can imagine. Once you own a stylus (available at art and craft stores), begin collecting stencils so that you can make truly special cards for any occasion.

Instead of using theme paper, customize plain paper for specific occasions with special tie-ons, ribbons, and cards.

using wrapping paper

Paper is probably the most basic and often used wrapping supply, so choose it with care. Rolls are preferable to folded sheets, since they accommodate more package sizes, there's less waste, and you won't have to worry about unsightly folds. Printed wraps can be an easy solution for special occasions, but they rarely have much individuality and are costly to boot.

Plain paper, in either rich colors or gutsy neutrals, perhaps with an interesting texture, will provide a much more sympathetic backdrop for your creativity, showcasing a stunning fabric ribbon or a package tie-on far more

effectively than a busy pattern would. 30- or 40-pound brown kraft paper in a 24"- or 30"-wide roll might be the answer to your basic wrapping paper needs. If possible, buy a 1,000-foot roll on a roll paper cutter: It will last forever, and it can be dressed up or down to suit the occasion—with tartan ribbon for sporty gifts, raffia for contemporary simplicity, or sheer gold ribbon for an elegant presentation. Though not technically a paper, cellophane is another very useful wrapping that can unify a collection of disparate elements or keep a multipart gift intact without obscuring its contents.

When cutting cellophane and wrapping paper, it's easier to *slide* the scissors than to use a cutting action. This makes a much smoother cut-line.

Enhance a book gift with an interesting presentation: Wrap it in a paper that reflects the subject or theme of the book, and add a tie-on that carries out the theme, too.

Shimmering Wraps

Metallic papers come in a glorious range of finishes and textures: matte and shiny, smooth and hammered; gold, silver, or copper. Depending on your choice of ribbons, cords, tie-ons, and other trims, you can make your package as tailored or as fancy as you like.

Maps as Wraps

Maps of all sizes make sensational wraps for gifts. For small packages, use the maps in the back of airline magazines, choose subway or bus maps, or buy an atlas and use the great variety of maps for lots of people on your list. For large packages, try road maps.

Choose your map wrap to reflect your gift recipient: a map that shows a home state or city, a real vacation destination, or a destination only dreamed of. For a far-flung friend, pick a map with *both* your cities on it and connect the two cities with a bold dotted line. Embellish the package with a compass, toy car, flag, state bird, or tokens for tolls.

This gift is wrapped in a map of Indiana and trimmed with a peony—the Indiana state flower.

A selection of vintage family photographs is copied on a dark background for uniquely personal gift wrap. A crimped metallic ribbon completes the package.

Personalized Wrapping Paper

You can distinguish your gift with personalized wrapping paper you've created especially for the occasion. Create a collage of photographs, trading cards, postcards, or other ephemera that will have meaning for the recipient. Devise a pleasing arrangement and photocopy the collage on a color copier. Vintage photos are particularly effective and the warm sepia color of old photographs reproduces handsomely on a color copier.

Most color copiers can print 11″ × 17″ sheets, ideal for wrapping small or medium-size gifts. If you create a random pattern, you'll be able to overlap two or more sheets, for wrapping larger presents. It's significantly less expensive to make color copies in multiples, so make at least several copies.

Simply arrange your items face down on the bed of a color copier. If you like, place a sheet of background paper face down over the photos; this will give you a colored or patterned background instead of a white background. Close the cover of the copier and print.

using fabric as wrap

When we think of wrapping we tend to think paper. In fact, fabric is often a better choice, particularly for large or oddly shaped items. It can be much wider than the standard 360 paper roll—up to 1080 in the case of tulle. It's also a good way to use remnants left over from decorating or dressmaking projects. And people are always dazzled by a fabric wrapping; it seems elegant and more professional somehow.

It's not necessary to have any sewing skills to use fabric wraps, but you should finish the raw edges in some way for the prettiest look. Cutting your piece to size with pinking or craft shears gives a decorative effect to the raw edges, or if the fabric is loosely woven you can simply pull several rows of threads to create a fringe.

This wrap is reminiscent of the Japanese technique and can be reused over and over. It's a great way to dress up a costly bottle of wine for a particularly notable birthday or anniversary.

Fringe the edges of a 30" square of fabric. Stand the bottle in the middle of the square. Bring two opposite corners of the fabric to the top of the bottle; tie in a double knot. Cross the remaining two corners over the back of the bottle and around to the front; tie in a double knot.

how to wrap a box

WRAPPING LARGE GIFTS

When you want to wrap something very large, try one of these materials:

- *Paper tablecloths* are inexpensive and large: about four feet wide. Save leftover scraps for wrapping smaller gifts.
- *Fabric* can be purchased in several widths and any length. Pleat it, fold it, treat it as if it were paper. Use it for making big bows, too.
- *Tulle* (netting) comes in great colors. It's inexpensive, lightweight, easy to use, and easy to store.
- *Cellophane* is available in wide rolls. Wrap your package first in some other material, then cover it with cellophane for a professional look.

These precise directions are for a 9½" × 15½" box. But since your box may be a different size and shape, use this formula for estimating the amount of wrapping paper you'll need: For the length of paper, it's the box length plus 2 times the box height plus 2". For the width of the paper, it's the circumference of the box plus 3" for overlapping plus 1" for folding under.

Determine the optimum placement of a gift box on the wrapping paper before you cut the paper to size. Small boxes can be placed across the width of the paper; large ones may require the length. If there's a design on the paper, consider how it will fall on the box; if it's very strong, try to center it on the box top.

what you'll need

- 1 box, 9½" × 15½" × 2"
- 1 piece of wrapping paper, 28" × 22"
- Transparent tape
- Double-stick tape
- 1 piece of ribbon or cord, 2½ yards long

how to do it

1. Center the box, top down, on the wrong side of the paper. Wrap the paper around the box, bringing it to the bottom of the box. Tape the underflap of the paper to the box to hold it in place while you make a tight wrap.
2. Fold under 1" or 2" of the top edge of the paper to create a neat overlap, and secure with 4" of double-stick tape. This folded edge should fall near the center of the back of the box.
3. With the box still top down, fold in the paper on the sides of either end of the box and gently crease along the sides of the box, as shown in the illustration. This will create the end flaps.
4. At one end, crease the flap on the bottom of the box (which is actually on top right now), and then fold the remaining flap up to enclose the end of the box. Fold in ½" of the flap to make a neat edge, and secure

to the back of the box with double-stick tape. Repeat at the other end of the box. If you have a very deep box, the flaps should end just below the center of the box depth.

5. To tie a simple bow, begin by grasping the ribbon or cord 12″ from one end; this end will later become a loop for the bow. Hold the ribbon centered on the top of the box, slightly above the middle.
6. Wrap the long end of the ribbon around the length of the box, bring it to the front, and twist the ribbon 90 degrees where it intersects with the short end.
7. Now wrap the long end of ribbon around the width of the box, slip the end under the intersection, and tie a knot on top of the box. The ribbon is flat on the bottom of the box and knotted where you'll either tie the bow, add a larger bow, or add a tie-on decoration.
8. Tie a bow shoelace style, and finish the ribbon ends in a V-cut or on a slant, to the desired lengths.

Don't get fixated on perfection: Wrap with thought and care, and the results will be wonderful. Remember that giving gifts is supposed to be a joyous activity.

To Paula

how to tie a bow

This bow, commonly called a "florist's bow," takes practice, but once you master the technique you'll use it often. These instructions are for making a 5" bow with eight loops, but you may adapt this technique to make a flatter bow with only four loops or a full pom-pom bow with twelve to sixteen loops. This bow is easiest to make with double-face ribbon. If you use single-face ribbon, you must twist the ribbon after each loop is formed, so the right side faces out.

what you'll need

- 1 piece of ribbon, 60" long
- Thin wire
- Fabric scissors

how to do it

1. Start in the middle of the ribbon, 30" from either end. Make a loop over your thumb, pinching the crisscross between your thumb and index finger.
2. Make a loop using about 6½" of ribbon, and pinch as you did in step 1.
3. Alternating sides, make a total of 8 loops (4 loops made from each long end of ribbon).
4. Slip a piece of thin wire through the loop you made over your thumb, and secure the bow loops you are holding by twisting the wire tightly around them. Adjust the loops evenly.
5. Trim the ends of the ribbon: Either fold each ribbon end in half and cut at a 45-degree angle from the ribbon edge to the fold to create a V-cut, or cut at an angle.

embossed tags

Fold a piece of paper in half to make a tag. Open the tag and, holding it up to a lamp or window for backlighting, position the stencil on the right side of the front of the tag in the desired location. Tape it in place.

Now turn the open tag over and, working from the wrong side, use the stylus to emboss the paper by first outlining each element and then applying the stylus to the interior of each element. This will create a raised design on the front of the tag. If you like, color the embossed design with markers or paint. Punch a hole in the upper left-hand corner of the tag and thread a string or ribbon through.

elegant embossing

The embossing technique that works beautifully for cards also lends itself to stylish and sophisticated wrapping paper. It is a little more difficult to work with larger pieces of paper, but patience and practice will yield exquisite results. You may choose to emboss designs at random on a light- to medium-weight paper, or you may engineer a very specific design for someone special on your list. Follow the directions below to create an embossed paper with your needs in mind.

what you'll need

- Wrapping paper
- Photograph
- Piece of cardboard several inches larger than the photograph
- 1″-wide burnishing tool
- Alphabet stencil
- Embossing stylus
- Glue for paper

how to do it

1. Wrap the gift in the wrapping paper (see page 109), but do not tape the paper. Gently crease the edges so that you can easily see the outline of the box top—this is the area that will be embossed. Remove the paper and smooth it out, right side up.
2. Measure the height and width of your photograph, and add ½″ to each dimension. Use these measurements to draw a rectangle in the center of the cardboard. If your photo is 3½″ × 5″, the rectangle should be 4″ × 5½″. Cut out and discard the rectangle; the remaining piece of cardboard, with the rectangular cutout, is your template.
3. Place the template under the wrapping paper, a little above center. Still working from the right side of the paper, gently use the burnishing tool to emboss the cutout rectangle.

4. Now turn the paper over so the wrong side is facing you. Position the alphabet stencil, also wrong side up, under the paper below the indented rectangle. Use the stylus to indent the desired letters; they will appear embossed from the right side.
5. Glue the photograph to the face of the paper, centering it in the rectangle. Fit the paper onto the box, and tape tightly in place.

An old or recent photograph of Dad is the focus of this unique and individual gift wrap, so be sure to pick a snapshot of him at his handsomest. He'll be thrilled and flattered at the trouble you've taken with his gift.

holding it all

Boxes make convenient and easy-to-wrap holders for gifts, but they are hardly the entire story when it comes to packing up your gift. Discount stores, hardware stores, housewares departments, and craft shops all offer containers that can be dressed up or down to suit your gift, and often they cost no more than a standard cardboard box. Here are just a few ideas to get you thinking "outside the box."

MAKING MAGNETS

Craft supply stores sell sheets of magnetized flexible vinyl with adhesive and a protective backing on one side. To turn a favorite photo, card, or magazine picture into a decorative magnet, rough-cut a piece of magnetized vinyl large enough to accommodate your chosen image. Peel off the backing and press the image onto the adhesive. Use very sharp scissors to cut around the image, cutting through the vinyl sheet as well.

FLOWER POT CONTAINERS

Terra-cotta pots make special containers for presenting gifts. They are inexpensive, available in virtually any size, and can be reused for plants, or passed along with yet another gift inside. Stow your gift in the pot and top it with a matching saucer for the lid. For added security, tape the saucer in four places before tying the ribbon to hide the tape. Follow directions on page 111 to add a festive bow on top.

MAGNETIC BOXES

Don't overlook the possibilities the metallic surfaces of galvanized tin boxes, recipe files, strongboxes, or file boxes provide for using magnetic embellishments.

Contrast the metallic finish of the box with a soft taffeta bow, and add a collection of purchased or homemade magnets. A magnetic bulldog clip from a stationer cleverly attaches a greeting card to the tin box.

JEWELS FROM THE SEA

A gift of jewelry begs for an exquisite presentation. A large bivalve shell, such as a sculptured clamshell, makes a handsome container for a strand of pearls or a pair of earrings; tie the shell closed with narrow ribbon, cord, or wire. A ring will fit into a small bivalve or nest of tissue paper if you like. A medium-size scallop shell is perfect for a larger ring or a pair of earrings.

bridal shower bouquet

This is a delightful gift to give the bride at a shower or to give as a prize at a shower—or both! Hiding under the pretty netting and silk flowers is a Tupperware double colander that any cook would love.

what you'll need

- Tupperware double colander, shallow pan, or skillet with lid
- 1¼ yards white crepe paper
- 1 yard 72″-wide netting, cut in half to make two 36″ squares
- 2 pieces of white wire-edge ribbon, each 1¼ yards long
- Silk flowers and greenery

how to do it

1. Cover the assembled colander with crepe paper, tucking in the sides and gathering the excess at the top of the colander handle.
2. Layer the two squares of netting. Center the wrapped colander on the netting. Wrap the netting around the colander, gathering it at the top of the colander handle.
3. Tie one piece of ribbon around the gathers, making a half knot. With the second piece of ribbon, make a figure-eight-style bow of four equal loops and two tails. Place the bow over the half knot and secure the bow by finishing the knot. Adjust the loops and tails; V-cut the ends of the ribbons. To decorate the gift, tuck the stems of the silk flowers and greenery under the ribbon.

You may choose to create this bridal bouquet wrap to house yet another gift. Place your extra surprise inside the colander or lidded skillet, adding tissue or crinkled filler paper to protect the gift.

GIFT ON A STICK

Small boxed gifts are more festive when fastened to a wooden stick and then wrapped in colorful tissue paper, with a layer of cellophane to add sparkle, and pretty ribbons for decoration. These feature, from left to right, curling ribbon, two pieces of grosgrain ribbon, and wired novelty ribbon.

A SPECIAL WRAP FOR TOYS

The squares of an alphabet-and-number puzzle play mat make spectacular wraps for children's gifts. This is one way to create a package that's as colorful and playful as what's inside—and don't be surprised if the recipient prefers the box to its contents!

Play mats are made up of 36 squares—*A* to *Z* and 0 to 9—which will yield six boxes (six squares per box); the interior of each box is a 5¼″ cube.

If you like, pop the letter or number out of the top square and stand it upright.

LANTERNS

Festive, colorful paper lanterns make quick and easy containers for lightweight gifts. Because they store flat, the lanterns take up very little space in your gift-wrap pantry. Whether you are giving a silk scarf, a man's tie, or theater tickets, the lantern will add a special element of celebration to your present. The lantern at left is filled with individually wrapped fortune cookies for a hostess gift.

PAINT CANS

If you know someone who just loves red—or blue or pink or green—this is the gift wrap to do for her next big occasion. Buy an unused aluminum gallon paint can from your local paint store. Use a stencil to draw the letters *R, E, D* on a piece of red paper or adhesive-backed red vinyl, referring to the photograph for guidance; cut out the letters. If you use red paper, use spray adhesive to attach it to the paint can; if you use vinyl, peel off the protective backing and press the vinyl in place on the paint can.

Put together a collection of small red gifts—a red pen, red paper clips, red address book, red heart stickers, pretty red pin or earrings, cinnamon red hots, red hair ornaments, and so on. Wrap each one in silver paper and tie with red cord. Pile the gifts in the paint can in a bed of crinkled red filler paper.

MAGIC IN MINUTES

Gift Sacks

Here's a quick and easy technique for packaging gifts in a lighthearted, whimsical way. You need paper bags, a paper punch, and a slew of nifty tie-ons for decoration.

Wrap your gift in tissue paper or put filler paper in the gift bag. Close the bag and fold it back 2″ from the top edge. With a paper punch, make two holes through all layers; the placement of the holes depends on the decoration you're using—2″ apart for a cord or ribbon, for instance, one hole above the other for a silk flower. Attach the tie-on.

To Keith
To Jennifer

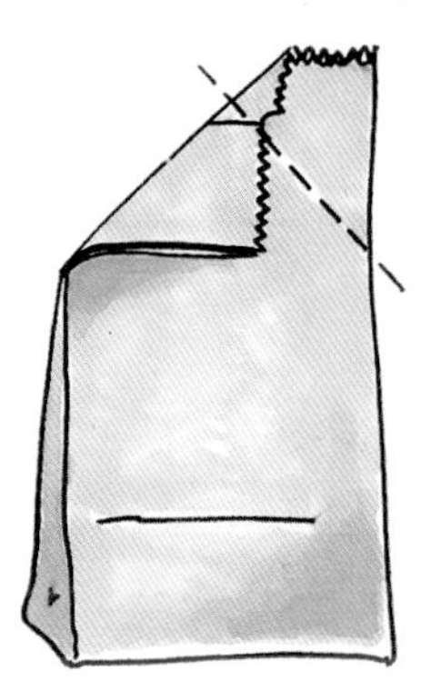

RESOURCES

This section offers information about birthstones and flowers of the month, as well as the zodiac, both Western and Eastern, to assist in the gift selection process. If you need to select a gift for a person born on February 17, 1963, for instance, you can quickly learn a good bit about the recipient:

- Her birth flower is the violet.
- The amethyst is her birthstone.
- She was born under the Western sign of Aquarius.
- She was born in the Chinese year of the rabbit.
- Her semiprecious stone is amazonite.

Guided by this information, you can see many ways that you could personalize your gift and its presentation:

- Send a bouquet of violets, with or without the fur!
- Select jewelry with amethyst stones or a costume jewelry interpretation.
- Give a carved stone or porcelain rabbit.
- Choose a sterling pendant with the Aquarius sign.
- Choose violet-colored or -printed gift-wrap paper.
- Tie a beautiful bouquet of silk violets on top of the package.
- Wrap the gift and fasten with wire to hold an amazonite stone.

The resource guide lists excellent mail-order sources for the *best* bread, brownies, foie gras, cookies, fruit, jams, bulbs, papers, ribbons, and craft supplies. Now you don't have to be a clever cook or a great gardener to present beautiful flowers or food.

In order to give exactly the right gift, you need to know all about the recipient. Use the gift registry on page 128 to keep track of information pertinent to the people in your life, so that when it's time to give a gift, you'll be full of great ideas. Make copies of this gift registry page, fill in the facts, and jot down any special wishes your friends and relatives happen to mention. Be prepared!

DATES AND GEMS OF THE ZODIAC

WESTERN ZODIAC

ARIES
March 21 to April 19
red jasper

TAURUS
April 20 to May 20
agate

GEMINI
May 21 to June 21
tigereye

CANCER
June 22 to July 22
aventurine

LEO
July 23 to August 22
crystal

VIRGO
August 23 to September 22
rose quartz

LIBRA
September 23 to October 23
smoky quartz

SCORPIO
October 24 to November 21
carnelian

SAGITTARIUS
November 22 to December 21
sodalite

CAPRICORN
December 22 to January 19
snowflake obsidian

AQUARIUS
January 20 to February 18
amazonite

PISCES
February 19 to March 20
amethyst

EASTERN ZODIAC

YEAR OF THE RAT
1924, Feb. 5–Jan. 23, 1925
1936, Jan. 24–Feb. 10, 1937
1948, Feb. 10–Jan. 28, 1949
1960, Jan. 28–Feb. 14, 1961
1972, Feb. 15–Feb. 2, 1973

YEAR OF THE OX
1925, Jan. 24–Feb. 12, 1926
1937, Feb. 11–Jan. 30, 1938
1950, Feb. 17–Feb. 5, 1951
1961, Feb. 15–Feb. 4, 1962
1973, Feb. 3–Jan. 22, 1974

YEAR OF THE TIGER
1926, Feb. 13–Feb. 1, 1927
1938, Jan. 31–Feb. 18, 1939
1949, Jan. 29–Feb. 16, 1950
1962, Feb. 5–Jan. 24, 1963
1974, Jan 23–Feb. 10, 1975

YEAR OF THE RABBIT
1927, Feb. 2–Jan. 22, 1928
1939, Feb. 19–Jan. 7, 1940
1951, Feb. 6–Jan. 26, 1952
1963, Jan. 25–Feb. 12, 1964
1975, Feb. 11–Jan. 30, 1976

YEAR OF THE DRAGON
1928, Jan. 23–Feb. 9, 1929
1940, Feb. 8–Jan. 26, 1941
1952, Jan. 27–Feb. 13, 1953
1964, Feb. 13–Feb. 1, 1965
1976, Jan. 31–Feb. 17, 1977

YEAR OF THE SNAKE
1929, Feb. 10–Jan. 29, 1930
1941, Jan. 27–Feb. 14, 1942
1953, Feb. 14–Feb. 2, 1954
1965, Feb. 2–Jan. 20, 1966
1977, Feb. 18–Feb. 6, 1978

YEAR OF THE HORSE
1930, Jan. 30–Feb. 16, 1931
1942, Feb. 15–Feb. 4, 1943
1954, Feb. 3–Jan. 23, 1955
1966, Jan. 21–Feb. 8, 1967
1978, Feb. 7–Jan. 27, 1979

YEAR OF THE GOAT
1931, Feb. 17–Feb. 5, 1932
1943, Feb. 5–Feb. 24, 1944
1955, Jan. 24–Jan. 11, 1956
1967, Feb. 9–Feb. 29, 1968
1979, Jan. 28–Feb. 15, 1980

YEAR OF THE MONKEY
1932, Feb. 6–Jan. 25, 1933
1944, Jan. 25–Feb. 12, 1945
1956, Feb. 12–Jan. 30, 1957
1968, Jan. 30–Feb. 16, 1969
1980, Feb. 16–Feb. 4, 1981

YEAR OF THE ROOSTER
1933, Jan. 26–Feb. 13, 1934
1945, Feb. 13–Feb. 1, 1946
1957, Jan. 31–Feb. 17, 1958
1969, Feb. 17–Feb. 5, 1970
1981, Feb. 5–Jan. 24, 1982

YEAR OF THE DOG
1934, Feb. 14–Feb. 3, 1935
1946, Feb. 2–Jan. 21, 1947
1958, Feb. 18–Feb. 7, 1959
1970, Feb. 6–Jan. 25, 1971
1982, Jan. 25–Feb. 12, 1983

YEAR OF THE PIG
1935, Feb. 4–Jan. 23, 1936
1947, Jan. 22–Feb. 9, 1948
1959, Feb. 8–Jan. 27, 1960
1971, Jan. 26–Feb. 14, 1972
1983, Feb. 13–Feb. 1, 1984

FLOWERS AND BIRTHSTONES

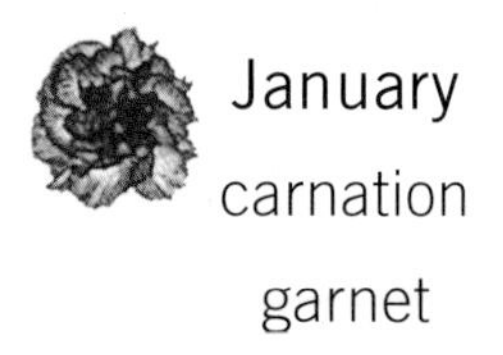

January
carnation
garnet

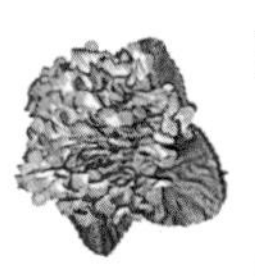

February
violet
amethyst

March
jonquil
aquamarine

April
sweet pea
diamond

May
lily of the valley
emerald

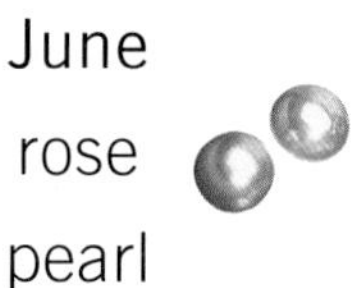

June
rose
pearl

July
larkspur
ruby

August
gladiolus
peridot

September
aster
sapphire

October
calendula
opal

November
chrysanthemum
topaz

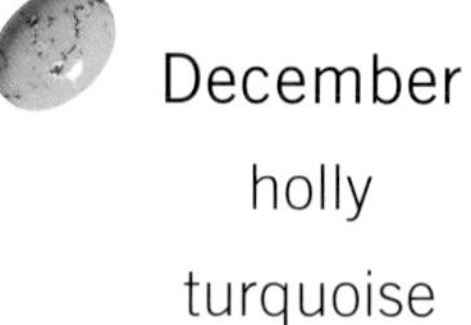

December
holly
turquoise

ANNIVERSARY GIFTS

ANNIVERSARY	TRADITIONAL	MODERN
1st	paper	clocks
2nd	cotton	china
3rd	leather	crystal and glass
4th	fruit and flowers, linen	electrical appliances
5th	wood	silverware
6th	sugar and sweets, iron	wood
7th	wool, copper	desk sets
8th	bronze, rubber	linens, lace
9th	pottery, willow	leather
10th	tin, aluminum	diamond jewelry
11th	steel	fashion jewelry
12th	silk, fine linen	pearls, colored gems
13th	lace	textiles, furs
14th	ivory	gold jewelry
15th	crystal	watches
20th	china	platinum
25th	silver	sterling silver
30th	pearls, ivory	diamonds
35th	coral, jade	jade
40th	rubies	rubies
45th	sapphires	sapphires
50th	gold	gold
55th	emeralds	emeralds
60th	diamonds	diamonds

RESOURCE GUIDE

FLOWERS

B BROOKS FINE FLOWERS
Call: 1-888-346-3356
www.bbrooks.com
Consortium of the finest florists in the world

CAROLINA SEEDS
P.O. Box 2658
Boone, NC 28607
Call: 1-800-825-5477
Fax: (828) 297-3888
www.carolinaseeds.com
Catalog—Large selection of seeds

COMPANION PLANTS
7247 N. Coolville Ridge
Athens, OH 45701
Call: (740) 592-4643
Fax: (740) 593-3092
www.frognet.net/companion_plants/
Catalog—Herbs

J & M HOME AND GARDEN
201 Main Street
Madison, NJ 07940
Call: (973) 377-4740
(800) 567-5268
www.jmhomegarden.com
Retail store

WAYSIDE GARDENS CO.
P.O. Box 1
Hodges, SC 29695
Call: 1-800-845-1124
Catalog—Bulbs

WHITE FLOWER FARM
P.O. Box 50
Litchfield, CT 06759-0050
Call: 1-800-503-9624
www.whiteflowerfarm.com
Catalog—The Garden Book

FOOD

ACME BREAD COMPANY
2730 Ninth, at Pardee
Berkeley, CA 94710
Call: (510) 843-2978
Bread

BALDUCCI'S
42-26 13 Street
Long Island City, NY 11101
Call: 1-800-225-3822
www.balducci.com
Catalog—For the gourmet pantry

BLACK HOUND NEW YORK
111 North 10 Street
Brooklyn, NY 11211
Call: 1-800-344-4417
www.blackhoundnewyork.com
Mail order catalog—Chocolate truffles and baked goods

D'ARTAGNAN
399-419 St. Paul Avenue
Jersey City, NJ 07306
Call: 1-800-327-8246
Best foie gras

DEAN & DELUCA
560 Broadway
New York, NY 10012
Call: 1-800-221-7714
Fax: 1-800-781-4050
www.deandeluca.com
Retail store—Fine food, cooking supplies, kitchenware

FAIRYTALE BROWNIES
Call: 1-800-324-7982
www.brownies.com
Mail order—Baked with premium Callebaut chocolate

GODIVA
139 Mill Rock Road East
Suite 2
Old Saybrook, CT 06475
Call: 1-800-946-3482
www.godiva.com
Retail store

JUNIOR'S CHEESECAKE, INC.
386 Flatbush Avenue
Brooklyn, NY 11201
Call: 1-888-577-2253
Fax: (718) 260-9849
www.juniorscheesecake.com
Freshest, most delicious cheesecake

MANHATTAN FRUITIER
105 East 29 Street
New York, NY 10016
Call: (212) 686-0404
Catalog—Fruit and savories

NEIMAN MARCUS BY MAIL
P.O. Box 650589
Dallas, TX 75265-0589
Call: 1-800-825-8000
www.neimanmarcus.com
Mail order catalog—Fine foods

OLD CHATHAM SHEEP HERDING COMPANY
Shaker Museum Road
Old Chatham, NY 12136
Call: 1-888-743-3760
Mail order—Cheeses

WILLIAMS-SONOMA
Mail Order Department
P.O. Box 7456
San Francisco, CA 94120-7456
Call: 1-800-541-2233
Fax: (702) 363-2541
Catalog—For cooks

OTHER GIFTS

AGATHA
158 Spring Street
New York, NY 10012
Call: (212) 925-7701
Fax: (212) 925-7617
Mail order: 1-888-242-8427
Retail store—Jewelry

AMAZON.COM
Web site—Books, music, toys

THE ART INSTITUTE OF CHICAGO
The Museum Shop
Michigan Ave. at Adams St.
Chicago, IL 60603
Call: 1-800-621-9337
www.artic.edu/aic./shops

BAS BLEU INC.
Bookseller-By-Post
515 Means Street, N.W.
Atlanta, GA 30318
Call: 1-800-433-1155
Fax: (404) 577-6626
www.basbleu.com
Mail order catalog—Books

BESTSELECTIONS.COM
Web site—collections of luxury goods from shops around the world

BLISS SPA
568 Broadway
Suite 207
New York, NY 10012
Call: (212) 219-8970
Fax: (212) 965-1433
www.blissworld.com
Spa and catalog

GEARYS OF BEVERLY HILLS
9 Gearys Drive
Cranston, RI 02920-4483
Call: 1-800-243-2797
Fax: 1-800-295-1880
Retail store—Gifts

L'ART DE VIVRE
3342 Melrose Avenue, N.W.
Roanoke, VA 24017
Call: 1-800-411-6515
www.lartdevivre.com
Mail order catalog—Gifts

MERRIMADE
185 Plains Road
Suite 301E
Milford, CT 06460-2474
Call: 1-800-344-4256
Catalog—Fine stationery and gifts

THE METROPOLITAN MUSEUM OF ART STORE
255 Gracie Station
New York, NY 10028-9998
Call: 1-800-468-7386
www.metmuseum.org

THE MUSEUM OF MODERN ART
11 West 53 Street
New York, NY 10019
Call: (212) 708-9400
www.moma.org

MUSEUM OF FINE ARTS, BOSTON
P.O. Box 244
Avon, MA 02322-0244
Call: 1-800-225-5592
www.mfa.org/shop

PROFESSIONAL CUTLERY DIRECT
242 Branford Road
North Branford, CT 06471
Call: 1-800-859-6994
www.cutlery.com
Catalog—Chef's essential

RESTORATION HARDWARE
104 Challenger Drive
Portland, TN 37148-1703
Call: 1-800-762-1005
Fax: (615) 325-1398
www.restorationhardware.com
Retail store

SEND.COM
Web site—Gifts, liquor, flowers and more

THE SOURCE PERRIER COLLECTION
P.O. Box 3500
Forrester Center, WV 25438
Call: 1-888-543-2804
www.perrier.com
Mail order catalog—Home and garden

WRAPPING & RIBBONS

ALLEN PAPER & SONS, INC.
242 Ridgedale Avenue
Morristown, NJ 07962-1262
Call: (973) 538-4826
Fax: (973) 538-1288
Kraft paper and corrugate

C.M. OFFRAY & SON, INC.
Route 24, Box 601
Chester, NJ 07930-0601
Call: (908) 879-4700
Major source for ribbons and ribbon trims

KATE'S PAPERIE
8 West 13 Street
New York, NY 10011
Call: (212) 633-0570
Fax: (212) 941-9560
Retail store—Catalog
Stationer and wrapping paper

WONDER WOOD
P.O. Box 659
Mancos, CO 81328
Call: 1-800-833-8573
Catalog—Excelsior (retail and bulk sizes)

DONATIONS

GOD'S LOVE WE DELIVER
Call: (212) 294-8138
www.glwd.org
Non-profit committed to delivering hot meals to home-bound HIV positive people

HEIFER PROJECT INTERNATIONAL
P.O. Box 8106
Little Rock, AR 72203-8106
Call: 1-800-422-0755
Fax: (501) 376-8906
www.heifer.org
Nonprofit organization that helps hungry people feed themselves, earn income and care for the environment

MAKE-A-WISH FOUNDATION
CALL: 1-800-722-WISH
Grants wishes to children with life-threatening medical conditions

SERRV INTERNATIONAL
CALL: 1-800-422-5915
www.serrv.org
Nonprofit program that promotes the social and economic progress of people in developing regions of the world by purchasing their crafts.

PERSONAL FAVORITES

PERSONAL GIFT REGISTRY

Name: ______________________
Address: ______________________
Phone: ______________________
E-mail: ______________________
Birthday: ______________________
Anniversaries: ______________________
Other Special Dates: ______________________
____
____
____

Favorites
Color: ______________________
Flower: ______________________
Food: ______________________
Music: ______________________
Hobbies: ______________________
Useful Information: ______________________
Gift Ideas: ______________________
____
____

Name: ______________________
Address: ______________________
Phone: ______________________
E-mai: ______________________
Birthday: ______________________
Anniversaries: ______________________
Other Special Dates: ______________________
____
____
____

Favorites
Color: ______________________
Flower: ______________________
Food: ______________________
Music: ______________________
Hobbies: ______________________
Useful Information: ______________________
Gift Ideas: ______________________
____
____

Name: ______________________
Address: ______________________
Phone: ______________________
E-mai: ______________________
Birthday: ______________________
Anniversaries: ______________________
Other Special Dates: ______________________
____
____
____

Favorites
Color: ______________________
Flower: ______________________
Food: ______________________
Music: ______________________
Hobbies: ______________________
Useful Information: ______________________
Gift Ideas: ______________________
____
____

BUS LINE